Color and Music in the New Age

Color and Music in The New Age

By
Corinne Heline

DeVorss and Company, *Publishers*
P.O. Box 550
Marina del Rey, CA 90294

Tenth Printing, 1985

ISBN: 0-87516-432-3

Printed in the United States of America

TABLE OF CONTENTS

PART I

Astrological Correlations

PART II

The Mystery of White and Black

PART III

New Age Developments

PART IV

Color and Music of the Four Sacred Seasons

George Frederic Handel's Messiah
Richard Wagner's Parsifal

Mendelssohn's Midsummer Night's Dream
Wagner's Die Meistersinger

PART ONE

ASTROLOGICAL CORRELATIONS

CHAPTER I

Color Significance of the Twelve Zodiacal Signs

Capricorn — January

apricorn is a mystery sign possessing profound depths and unlimited powers. Its colors (so-called) are black and white, for in it merge the mystery of darkest night and the glory of light supernal. The Sun's entrance into Capricorn marks the wonder of the year. Few, and especially favored, are those found worthy at this highly favored time to cross the bridge of darkness and, by virtue of the "Mighty Rite," to know the glory of the new-born Christ.

The labor of Hercules was to descend into Hades and capture the monster Cerebus. On this hazardous journey he was accompanied by Minerva and Mercury. Every aspirant must cross this bridge of darkness before he can stand in the radiation of the Great White Light; and always in the conquest of the monster (self) he is accompanied by Minerva and Mercury, the accumulation of soul-wisdom garnered from many earth pilgrimages.

Capricorn is the home of the Archangels. Chief among these is that glorious archangelic Being, the Christ. There are four mighty Star-Angels, second in power and majesty to Him only, who guard the gateways to the four Sacred Seasons, the two Equinoxes and the two Solstices. One of the four is Gabriel, the minister of love and compassion, who is guardian of the Winter Solstice. His pure white light suffuses Holy Night, and his encompassing under-

11

standing surrounds all earth's mothers and prospective mothers. He was the guardian and teacher of the world's most perfect mother, the Divine Virgin Mary, throughout her entire life. He guided her through the mystery and glory of her angelic Initiation, after which she was hailed as "Queen of Angels and of men."

In its highest aspect, black is not negative. It denotes mystery—that which is formless and working within, unperceived and unseen. The powerful White Ray is not concerned with physical healing but with spiritual illumination. Its focusing center within the human body-temple is the apex of the head, its forces playing through the pineal gland. The awakening of this center by means of the white light enables an aspirant to understand the true significance of St. Paul's words: "Till Christ be formed in you." When this center, and its polar opposite, the pituitary body, become illumined, they symbolically represent the positive and negative forces of Joseph and Mary; and the bridge which connects these two centers represents a veritable manger of light. When this occurs an aspirant is conscious of an inner quickening, the birth of the Christ within himself, and the spiritually charged time of the Winter Solstice has become in very truth a "Holy Night."

Early Rosicrucians taught their students how to surround themselves and others with the white light as a means of protection. No more perfect gift can we bestow upon our loved ones than to surround them with this aura of well-being.

Aquarius — February

Hercules was termed the *Good Shepherd of Greece.* He was the supreme Lord of the Divine Fire, and he came as the mediator between the old and a new age. His work for human regeneration was not through war and conquest but through teaching the precepts of the Golden Rule. His twelve labors outlined the stages of this work. Aquarius is the mediator between the old and the new. The keynote of Uranus, the Aquarian planet, is "Behold, I make all things new."

The Aquarian labor was the cleansing of the Augean stables which housed three thousand oxen, but had not been cleaned for thirty years. This task is attuned to the number 3, the number indicative of cleansing man's physical and emotional bodies and spiritualizing his mind. The accomplishment of this Herculean task is causing the widespread turmoil, conflict and devastation now afflicting the nations.

The Aquarian color is a clear, beautiful blue interspersed with silver lights. This is known by color therapists as Uranian or electric blue. It is the color especially helpful to inventors, particularly those working with electricity; also, by anyone working with any phase of New Age discoveries or inventions. Physically, this Uranian blue is recommended for acceleration of the respiratory system, so is most effective in cases of shortness of breath. Physically, it lifts one's consciousness into contact with new and hitherto undiscovered truths.

Aquarius promotes group work. Before uniting for group meditation or concerted activity of any kind, it is well for the group members to visualize individual and collective submergence in the Aquarian blue. The results of group meditation under the Aquarian Full Moon will be greatly enriched by maintaining such a sense of immersion in the Blue Ray as they concentrate on projecting its powerful vibration toward making "all things new" in world conditions and in the lives of every person and every living creature within the sphere of the group's influence—a service that fulfills the Aquarian zodiacal Hierarchy's ideal of oneness of the whole and wholeness of the one.

Pisces — March

The Piscean color is a soft azure, a misty blue combining the deep Jupiterian tone with that of the higher Neptunian octave since Jupiter and Neptune are co-rulers of Pisces. The Piscean Ray is effective for healing, particularly those diseases rooted in the emotions.

The labor of Hercules as related to Pisces was to capture the herd of red cattle belonging to the giant Geryones. This was a difficult task as the cattle were guarded by a huge two-headed monster. The herd typifies humanity: the monster materialism, that carnal power that threatens to dominate the world. In this aspect it represents the Old Order now passing. The Herculean labor is, therefore, indicative of the New Order striving to come to birth. Most of the conflict and turmoil now rampant springs from a struggle between the two for supremacy.

When Hercules (the power of Spirit) finally rescued the herd of cattle (humanity) from the vicious monster (materiality), his victory was rewarded by the gift of a golden bowl from the Sun God Helios. This bowl symbolizes the radiant soul-body which can be attained only by rendering loving, selfless service.

Aries — April

The Ray of Aries is red, the cosmic color of life. Hence red blood in the human body is the seat of the life energy. The first evidence of the transmutation of the lower bodily energies into higher spiritual forces appears in a brightening of the blood stream. The call constantly goes out to give blood for the saving of life; this widespread transfer of blood from those who are strong and healthy to the weak and wounded is a significant factor in the establishment of world brotherhood.

Color therapy reached a high degree of efficiency among the ancients, especially the Greeks. It was practically lost to modern healing science until it was "discovered" (really re-discovered) during World War II. Now, however, many hospitals and clinics are making extensive use of it and thus proving its effectiveness. During the war large numbers of soldiers suffering the numbing effects of fear and shell-shock began to take notice of their immediate environment after a few days in a room decorated in red; although some of them had refused food for days, their appetites soon returned.

The keynote of Aries is activity. This activity manifests on the material plane as ambition, initiative, creativeness; on the higher plane, as spiritual adventuring and pioneering along lines looking toward a better world for all humanity.

Red appears at the base of the spectrum. It vibrates to middle C in the musical scale and is the most stimulating of all colors. Mars is the governing planet of Aries, and the color of Mars is red. Since the Sun in Aries is white, natives of the latter may run the entire gamut from red to white, from the lowest to the highest.

The Herculean Labor of Aries was to capture the man-eating horse belonging to Diomedes, son of the War God Mars. This horse, possessing iron hoofs and iron wings, sped over the earth with the speed of lightning, leaving death and destruction in its wake—a graphic description of modern military devastation. Hercules, the Christ of the Greeks, was a son of peace, and it is only the power of peace that can overcome the curse and destructiveness of war.

Taurus — May

During the Full Moon of the zodiacal Hierarchy of Taurus, the lunar orb pours out its blessings upon earth by means of its own particular Yellow Ray. Consider this Ray in its own cosmic setting and significance. In the spectrum there are three primary colors: blue, yellow and red. Blue belongs to the Father; yellow, to the Son or Christ; red, to the Holy spirit. In the life of man, these three aspects of Divinity are expressed in the principles of Will, Wisdom and Activity, respectively. The Will aspect of God manifests as the Blue Ray; the Wisdom aspect of Christ as the Yellow Ray; the Activity or Holy Ghost aspect as the Red Ray. Hence, potent indeed is the Yellow Ray for it is the principle through which the love and wisdom of the Lord Christ manifests here on earth.

The true function of wisdom is illumination of the mind through the power of love. Yellow is, therefore, the most powerful vibration for the treatment of all forms of mental affliction. It is also the Ray which bestows mental stimulation and spiritual inspiration. When psychology becomes a science of the psyche or soul as well as of the mind—as the word indicates—that Ray will be used not only for the healing of mental diseases but for spiritualizing, or Christing, the mind. This is the most important development at this stage of human evolution.

The Herculean labor of Taurus was overcoming the mighty Cretan Bull. This labor was long and arduous, for many times the vicious beast would get out from under Hercules' control and ravage the countryside, to the grief and distress of the people. Taurus is the most powerful of the three earth signs and is, therefore, most aptly represented by a bull.

Naturally, Taurean natives are closely attuned to the products of earth. The acquisition of material things comes easy to them, often leading to extravagance and prodigality. "I possess" is the keynote of Taurus; "I love" is the keynote of Venus, its planetary ruler. Before the "bull" in an aspirant's nature can be conquered, he must transmute the love of personal possessions into that self-sacrificing service which is the mark of an illumined Taurean.

During the month of May the increase and fertility of Taurus manifest throughout all nature. May brings forth from the "death" and barrenness of winter the colorful profusion of spring. Likewise, persistence and perseverence, qualities inherent in the spiritually awakened Taurean, will transmute self-seeking into self-less-ness and the tendency toward possessiveness into an impulse to share.

The Taurean labor exemplified in the story of Hercules is a particularly difficult task. By this hero's complete mastery, the Cretan Bull ceased to spread death and devastation. Instead, it turned its great strength toward cultivating the land, that increased productivity might bring peace and plenty to the people. So it is that peace, plenty and beauty become the soul signature of spiritually awakened Taureans.

Under the Taurus Hierarchy humanity is liquidating its karmic debts. Natives of this sign are likely to face a special measure of accumulated obligations. In fact, humanity at large is in the throes of karmic travail.

The supreme event in human evolution and world history was the coming of the Christ. Another event of epoch-making significance is imminent. As the Christ, the mighty Sun Spirit, again draws nearer and nearer to earth, many human hearts are being cleansed and human eyes are being opened through sorrow and suffering. More and more, individuals are beginning to sense something of His benign presence and to receive in ever-increasing measure the healing of His love and blessing. The present crisis is lifting mankind into the light of understanding and compassion. Above the roaring thunder of storm clouds may be heard the triumphant chorusing of seraphic Hosts as they proclaim again a promise uttered by an ancient sage: "But unto you that fear my name shall the Sun of righteousness arise with healing in his wings." (Mal. 4:2).

Gemini — June

The Full Moon of Gemini is the Christ moon because it marks the time of His Ascension. The color for Gemini is violet, the hue that predominates in all Temples where the Ascension Rite is commemorated. Violet is of an extremely high vibration that is both healing and soothing. It is particularly potent for the treatment of all forms of severe or acute pain. The Violet Ray is not only effective in cases of physical pain; but to those persons psychologically ill or suffering in any way from sorrow or distress, it brings comfort and relief. For this reason, numerous people who have been bereaved choose this color in preference to black as a sign of mourning.

Violet has the highest rate of vibration of any color in the spectrum, and it is the means whereby the next higher sevenfold color scale will be revealed to human sight. This will come when men can lift their visual faculty to the level referred to by St. Matthew when he said, "Blessed are your eyes for they see."

The Gemini labor of Hercules was to gather two golden apples of Hesperides which grew upon the Tree of Life. About the trunk of this tree was entwined a huge serpent to guard its sacred treasure. Herein is a semblance of the Garden of Eden story of a serpent appearing in the forbidden tree to tempt Eve with an apple. The Tree of Life is the perfected etheric body which man can fashion only by conservation and transmutation of the "serpent fire" within his physical body. When he has learned to function in this perfected etheric extension, never again will he know death. Rather, he will walk eternally in the realm of everlasting life. That is to say, he will have gained immortality—symbolized by Hercules' attainment of the golden apples growing upon the Tree of Life. This is the spiritual quest in which all humanity is engaged under the guidance of the Hierarchy of Gemini.

Gemini is the sign of duality. As the sign of the Twins it

represents the present phase of evolution, during which man alternates between life and death. Under the Law of Alternation, man experiences such contrasts as joy and sorrow, health and sickness, plenty and poverty, light and darkness. A Gemini native functioning under this law is ofttimes prone to lack fixity of purpose and so should cultivate the quality of persistence. A Gemini individual is fortunate indeed if he possesses a fixed *ascendant* (Leo, Aquarius, Taurus or Scorpio) as it will aid him greatly in setting the impress of firmness and definiteness upon his character.

When Hercules finally succeeded in conquering the serpent and attaining the golden apples, great streams of ambrosia poured forth from the sacred tree. This is the same tree described in the Book of Revelation where it states that the fruit of the tree is for the healing of all nations—a statement meaning that when man has perfected his own etheric body, he will be free from the Law of Alternation. As St. John writes: "There shall be no more death,. . . .neither shall there be any more pain." Such is also the meaning of the words of our Blessed Lord who said, "Whoever drinketh of the water that I shall give him shall never thirst; but the water that I shall give him shall be to him a well of water springing up into everlasting life."

Cancer — July

The earth is filled with the powers of each zodiacal sign through which the Sun passes. During the month of July these forces which stream forth from the sign Cancer are charged with beauty, inspiration and illumination. Cancer is one of the mother signs of the heavens. In its mystic waters are born the seeds of life which ensoul every form extant upon earth. Hence, Cancer is termed the Gateway of Life.

Green is this sign's predominant color, for green is the pulsating, vibrating color tone of life. It is the color note of this planet; therefore, green is the color of nature. It is the most soothing and restful vibration of the entire color scale, an antidote for all nervous derangements. Who does not know the revivification and exhileration that comes from a night spent in the open, inhaling the fragrant breath of great towering pines? Even an hour spent upon the grass of a lawn or in a park causes a renewing pulsation to flow through one's entire body.

Hospitals that make use of color therapy have "green rooms" for the treatment of nervous disorders. During the war many patients suffering from severe cases of shell-shock and unable to sleep for days at a time enjoyed relaxation and rest after a few hours in one of these green rooms. People suffering from over-wrought, tired nerves find surcease of strain and tension and become quiet and relaxed by sitting upon a vista of rolling green hills or a pattern of green shadows cast by leafy boughs swaying gently in a breeze.

Green is a secondary color. It is formed by a blending of blue, the creative color vibration of the Father, with yellow, the love and wisdom principle of the Christ (Sun). Hence, green gives us the true meaning of life as it is evolved by the will of God in union with the love and wisdom of the Christ.

The Herculean labor of Cancer was to capture the golden doe which was the most prized possession of the beautiful and chaste Moon Goddess, Diana. The Moon governs Cancer, and through this sign play the powerful forces of Jupiter and Neptune. The Moon governs man's physical body; Jupiter, his soul; Neptune, his spirit. The exalted spiritual forces which belong to Cancer climax in the glory of the the Summer Solstice. Then it is that the Gate of Initiation swings wide and aspirants enter upon the supreme quest of new birth. The glory of such new birth is represented by the golden doe, the most precious treasure of the Moon Goddess.

By this new birth an aspirant develops a revitalized, beautiful and chaste physical body, a veritable temple for the indwelling spirit, and comes into a higher soul impulse that will flower in creative artistic abilities. Through it he will gain divine illumination that reveals to him the wondrous mysteries of both heaven and earth.

Life and *love* are synonomous in spiritual realms. New birth on all planes of manifestation through the magic power of love is the transcendent message of the Full Moon in Cancer.

Leo — August

During the Full Moon of Leo there is gold in the air, there is gold on the earth, there is gold in the sky, for at this time the Hierarchy of Leo is pouring love into the earth through the instumentality of the Sun, and the Sun's Ray is gold. Gold—another way of designating the Orange Ray created by blending the Yellow Ray of wisdom with the Red Ray of activity—inspires activity based on wisdom. This Ray is a tremendously powerful force for breaking up all forms of crystalization, not only in man's physical body but in his etheric and astral bodies as well.

Divinity and *humility* are keynotes for meditation during the Leo Full Moon period. It is also a time for man to rededicate himself anew to service inspired by love and rendered in humility.

The ductless glands have their centers in the etheric or vital body. They are the doorways to the seven major spiritual centers that are sometimes called "Roses" or "Stars." These centers are located in the astral body. This close connection between them and the ductless glands accounts for much of the imperfect functioning of the latter, for there are few persons in our present state of evolution who do not suffer from mal-functioning of these glands at some time or other in their lives. As stated before, the Gold or Orange Ray is a powerful factor in breaking up crystallization, and thus removing impediments to proper functioning of the glands.

That glorious Archangel, the Christ, is the Spiritual Sun of the heavens. In the physical body of a disciple the heart is the sun-center of light for an illumined life. When awakened, the heart center has the appearance of a glorious golden rose with its beautifully luminous auric petals extending far out to form a golden halo about the disciple. This is the Golden Robe of Mastership. It is also the reason why the Buddhic brotherhood wears orange-yellow robes. The work of the blessed Lord Buddha is centered in this great love or heart ray.

Hercules was the Sun-Man of the Greeks. His Leo labor was slaying the Nemean Lion. Unable to do this with external weapons, he was compelled to slay the beast by means of his own inner force. From its skin he made himself a golden robe that rendered him immune to hate and discord in any form. The only way an aspirant can attune himself to the love Ray is to live a life of understanding and peace. Through love-inspired transmutation of negative emotions he surrounds himself with a luminous aura that is impervious to inharmony and evil.

The Leo labor is claiming many devotees in the world of today. Man's evolution has brought him to a place where his principal task is slaying the lion of self. A long and arduous one it is, one which accounts for much of the current unrest, discord and con - flict. Through the conquest of self, however, pioneers of the New Age are becoming Sun-men in whom love is "the fulfilling of the law." In other words, relationships between individuals, govern - ments, nations and races are on the way to being centered in lov - ing understanding.

The Hierarchy of Leo holds before disciples one supreme ideal for attainmnet, an ideal which is the high theme for meditation on the night of the Full Moon in Leo. That ideal is to become worthy to stand in the presence of the Lord of Love and Light, the Blessed Christ, and receive His benediction in the words: "Well done, thou good and faithful servant . . . enter thou into the joy of thy lord."

Virgo — September

Mundane astrology teaches that Virgo and its planetary ruler Mercury are the sign and planet respectively of *reason*. Spiritual astrology, however, maintains that the highest aspect of both is *wisdom*. Mercury not only rules Virgo but is exalted in this sign. No aspirant can ever fully realize the effects of the exaltation of Mercury in Virgo until he has developed wisdom within himself.

King Solomon, considered the wisest of all earthly kings, admonished his people to get both knowledge and understanding, for a blending of the two produces wisdom. Knowledge and reason are products of the concrete mind; whether expressed through the written or spoken word, the findings of knowledge engendered by reason alone are cold and lifeless. Only when illumined by wisdom are they productive of inspiration.

The attainment of true wisdom ever leads an aspirant along the narrow path of renunciation. Christ Jesus admonished: "If any man will come after me, let him deny himself, and take up his cross daily, and follow me." An Illumined One of our own time has said that before a pupil can stand in the presence of the Master, his feet must be washed in the blood of his heart.

The labor of Hercules relative to Virgo was to gain the magic girdle possessed by the queen of the Amazons. A girdle encircles one's body and therefore symbolizes a protective aura of light surrounding a worthy aspirant. The proper noun *Amazon* means strong or powerful. A queen represents the soul. Wisdom, product of expanded soul-consciousness, is man's strongest and most powerful attribute. Reason deals with externals; wisdom is of the innermost heart of being.

Reasoning from appearance that the queen (soul) had deceived him when she promised to give him her girdle (protective aura), Hercules slew her. Entrance into the Temple of Light can never be gained by reason alone. Only to wisdom do the portals swing wide so a disciple may enter and partake of eternal life.

The color Ray of Virgo is purple. To it has been assigned royalty and "kingly sorrow." It is a blending of the Red Ray of activity with the Blue Ray of Divinity. As the red of one's lower nature is overcome and purified by the blue of his spirit, does a disciple understand the deep significance of the Purple Ray. It is then recognized as the supreme agency of purification.

The purple vibration is most effective in treating all diseases arising from impurities in the blood, such as eczema, boils, and so forth. It also alleviates fevers and swellings of various types, and is most stimulating to the entire glandular system.

When a disciple's lower nature is purified and sublimated by an infusion of spirituality, he is worthy to wear "the purple robe." He thus becomes a Son of the King. As such, he is able to manifest the real significance of the Lord Christ's statement to the effect that "All things that my Father hath are mine." These words convey the highest meaning of the exaltation of Mercury in Virgo, the ultimate goal at the end of the Path.

Libra — October

Yellow is the color wherewith the Hierarchy of Libra suffuses the earth while the Sun is transiting this sign. Yellow is a primary color, one of the holy trinity of colors which is composed of blue, yellow and red. The color yellow has tremendous potency and bears the signature of wisdom and peace. Also, it possesses great power to calm and soothe.

Libra is an airy sign and air is correlated with the mind. Therefore, yellow is of great benefit in conditions marked by disturbed, restless or unbalanced mental states. At no distant date mental institutions will incorporate color into their regular healing therapy. Wards done in tones of yellow will prove of great benefit in the treatment of violent patients.

In these days of stress and tension, when all the world seems to live dangerously near the brink of unthinkable calamities, it would be well if every house could have a yellow room; or, at least, a small alcove done in this color that is set aside for daily periods of prayer and meditation by every member of the family. Nervous and emotional children would be particularly susceptible to this soothing and healing influence, even though too young to understand the value of prayer and meditation. A story could be read to them or some picture shown that would serve to focus their attention as they benefited from the color influence. A person suffering from insomnia will get help from wearing yellow sleeping apparel, and anyone subject to depression or melancholia could have a yellow corner in his garden furnished with an easy chair. It is impossible to watch a mass of yellow poppies dancing in the Sun without feeling a new impulse of inspiration.

The Herculean labor of Libra was the capture of a wild boar, an extremely fierce and dangerous animal that lived upon precipitious and dizzy heights. Its capture was finally accomplished on the topmost peak of a snowy mountain crest. The wild boar symbolizes man's untamed lower propensities that can never be controlled until he climbs the heights of pure soul attainment.

Libra marks an important turning point in seasons of the year. As the Sun enters this sign the holy day of the Autumn Equinox is observed by students of mysticism throughout the world. At this time the earth is suffused with the descending Christ force. All nature reproduces, as it were, the glory light of this downpouring Christed power. Meadows and woodlands are adorned and made fragrant by yellow flowers, for yellow is Nature's predominant color during the month of October.

As Libra is the sign of an important turning point in Nature, so it is that the Autumn Equinox begins an important period of the life of mankind—for Libra is the trial gate or balance period of the year. At this time man stands before the harvest garnered from his deeds of the year drawing toward its close. He must be weighed in the balance and give a true karmic accounting for days and months just past.

Psychologists tell us that within man there are two forces in active operation, one tending toward self-assertion which leads to separateness; the other, toward love which leads to unity. These two forces are now struggling for supremacy within men and nations, and herein lies the cause of national and international transitional turmoil. Only as men and nations find the path leading to high peaks of soul attainment through the complete conquest of the lower and separative self, will the world be freed from its dark clouds of wars and rumors of wars. All humanity, individually and collectively, must pass through this trial gate of Libra and be tested to the uttermost. On one side of this gate stands Saturn, whose power is exalted in Libra. He holds within his hand the whiplash of karmic accounting, thus bringing sorrow, pain and purgation. On the other side stands Venus, ruler of Libra, pouring forth the wondrous power of love, that the reaping of no person or nation may be greater than can be borne. Venus also bestows tender benedictions of sympathy and compassion, thus tempering the wind to the shorn lamb.

Scorpio — November

Scorpio is one of the most powerful signs of the entire Zodiac. Its force is dual in aspect and extends from the lowest depths to the greatest heights; hence, it is symbolized by both a scorpion crawling on the ground and an eagle flying close to the Sun.

Scorpio's color is red, a clear, shining crimson. Students of color psychology make a mistake when they eschew red for it is one of the primary colors and it stimulates, accelerates and invigorates. It is only when red is mingled with tones of yellow and blackish gray that it is dangerous. The color red gives exhilaration by revitalizing all parts of the physical body.

When an esoteric student begins the work of transmutation—that is, purification of his animal nature and lifting its forces to a higher plane of expression—he should begin by using the clear, shining Ray of Scorpio red. In later processes he should make use of clear blue, while the transmutation must be completed under the purple-violet ray. Purple is a blending of red and blue.

The Scorpio labor was conquest of Hydra, a monstrous serpent with nine heads. Whenever Hercules cut off one of these heads, two appeared in its place. This is an apt and familiar symbol to every student working on transmutation. Finally, Hercules learned to place the dismembered heads under a *stone* and so completed the conquest. The *stone* stands for powers of mastership. In the temple of the human body the sacred stone is near the sacral plexus located at the base of the spine. This is where the sacred spinal fire lies coiled like a snake until it is awakened and lifted upward toward the head by the process of transmutation.

The sacral plexus is also red. But when this fire is lifted toward the mid-section of the body, it functions under the blue Ray. Then, as the spinal fire nears the spiritual centers in the head, its work is culminated under the purple-violet Ray.

Under the sign Scorpio meditation should be on the sublime work of transmutation, the highest attainment of that sign. Through transmutation the human body-temple ceases to be a "den of thieves" and becomes a true "house of prayer." One who accomplished this within himself gave the keyword for the Scorpio meditation. Again it was King Solomon, whose name means *Wisdom of the Sun.* Out of his own deep experience he declared: "He that is slow to anger is better than the mighty; and he that ruleth his spirit than he that taketh a city."

Sagittarius — December
Sagittarius is the sign of high idealism and noble aspirations. It

is represented pictorially by a figure that is half animal and half man, the latter drawing his bow and pointing an arrow at the stars. This pictograph symbolizes the divine spirit of animal-man aiming toward his potential godhood. In unregenerate Sagittarians the forces of heaven and earth are ever struggling for supremacy over one another. Its unpurified fire force excites lusts of the flesh while its higher aspect arouses a driving impulse to reach the heights.

Sagittarius is ninth of the twelve zodiacal signs. *Nine* is the number of man, and also of Initiation. The *five* factor is the perfected cube of spiritual attainment. A spiritualized mind is the highest expression for a Sagittarian. To such a Christed mentality all things are possible. The biblical keynote of this sign is given in the words of St. Paul: "Let this mind be in you, which was also in Christ Jesus." Sagittarius attains to its fullest expression in that great peace of mind which passes all understanding, and which comes only upon conquest of carnal desires and appetites.

The Sagittarian color is the deep, clear blue of a morning sea following a night of storm. This powerful blue Ray may be used for purification of one's physical body and illumination of one's mind. In New Age hospitals, where color will play such an important part in healing work, patients will be taught to suffuse their afflicted members in a "bath of color." When, through the power of visualization, groups of trained attendants perform such service for those who are unable to do it for themselves, they will make good use of this blue Ray.

Hercules' labor for this sign was to kill the man-eating birds of Stymphalis. These vicious fowl hovered over the marshes of Arcadia preying upon and devouring all that came their way. Arcadia denotes the pleasures of earthly life which would hold a Sagittarian in their grasp. The birds of Stymphalis are thoughts of lust and desire for power; thus, they are birds of prey rather than birds of liberation.

The most propitious time of the year for an aspirant to attain spiritual development is from the Autumn Equinox on September 21st to the Winter Solstice on December 21st. It is significant that during these three months the earth is suffused with the three primary colors of the spectrum: yellow, red and blue. During the month of October, when the golden Christ Ray is focussed upon our planet, the earth is bathed in yellow. In November, the month of Scorpio, the planetary color is red. In December, the Sagittarian month, blue predominates. These three primaries merge into the glorious white light on Holy Night.

When the Sun enters Sagittarius the Christian world celebrates the Advent Season. Each day of this season accelerates the upliftment of human consciousness. During an aspirant's preparation for the Holy Night Ritual, wherein he will stand in the presence of the "new born" Christ radiance, he will hear the jubilant chorusing of Angels and recognize within himself a glorious reflection of that Christed Light.

PART II

THE MYSTERY OF BLACK AND WHITE

CHAPTER II

The Presence and Absence of Color

oethe, who was, perhaps, the world's most profound color-scientist, thought that colors were the result of a mixture of darkness and light, of black and white. To show this he suggested an experiment in which a piece of white paper is placed on a black background and then viewed through a prism. Seen thus, colors appear, not on the white paper, but along the edges where the black and white meet.

The New Age color scheme will be something more than the traditional Newtonian spectrum. The Goethean peach-blossom has already entered the picture. Purple, like peach-blossom, is not found in the Newtonian spectrum, yet artists and others who are sensitive to color recognize that shadows and darkness are vibrant with colors of the higher range of the rainbow scale from blue through violet, and on into the purple which is seen in darkness.

White and black do, in truth, typify the epitome of creative activity. White represents the masculine or Father principle which manifests as divine life essence. Black typifies the feminine or form side of life. Life essence must have form through which to manifest in order to become visible on the physical plane. This feminine principle St. John describes as the *Logos or Word.* In the first chapter of his Gospel is given what is probably the most perfect formula of creation the world has ever received! "In the beginning was the Word, and the Word was with God and the Word was God. The same was in the beginning with God. All things were made by him; and without him was not anything made that was made."

All Color and No Color in Symbolism

The Path of Wisdom was outlined in the Egyptian Mysteries by a series of symbolic pictures. The spiritual enlightenment embodied in these symbols is so profound in its meaning that it belongs to no one period, race or religion, but to every serious student of truth at all times and in all places.

One of these ancient symbolic pictures depicts a high priest robed in white, emblem of purity. About his head is an aureole of golden radiance which bespeaks his high attainment. In one hand he holds a scepter pointing toward heaven; his other hand extends downward toward the earth. This symbol is saying that as man endeavors to ascend to the heavens, he must, at the same time, endeavor to conquer the material world below. The figure's waist is encircled by a girdle formed of a serpent biting its own tail—an emblem of eternity, for the high priest represents the masculine or Father principle of creation.

Another cipher shows a high priestess seated upon a throne placed between two pyramids, the one white and the other black. Her face is half-concealed by a dark veil, typifying the mysterious and secretive work always associated with the feminine phase of creation. Upon her breast appears a solar cross, representative of universal generation. On her knees rests an open papyrus, partly concealed by her mantle. This proclaims the fact that the most profound spiritual teachings are withheld from all who are not worthy to receive them.

Another of these picture-symbols is that of a man, blindfolded and walking toward a precipice where a huge crocodile with open mouth is waiting to devour him. He is weighted down by a heavy bundle which he carries over his shoulder, denoting the karmic debts wherewith he has burdened himself during past lives on earth. Above him is shown the Sun in partial eclipse, half in light and half in darkness. This picture depicts present-day humanity bearing its load of pain, poverty, suffering and sorrow as it wanders blindly and unknowingly toward possible destruction. However, mankind need not come to such an end. When man becomes wise enough to establish within himself a harmonious interaction between the masculine and feminine principles as typified by black and white, he will be led into the life more abundant. It is the present inharmonious relationship between these two principles that has plunged the world into its present confused and discordant state. Perfect balance between these two powers is known as *polarity*. When this balance has been attained, mankind will be able to build a new earth and a new heaven. We have stated repeatedly that the answer to the age-old question "What is truth?" may be summed up in that one word *polarity*.

L. Adams Beck, the famed feminine writer who wielded such a magic pen, gives expression to this profound assurance: "And when I fell asleep I dreamed this story in clear outline which I have since filled up until in my mind, at least, it has become a picture of man and woman as they are. There is no end to it—how could there be? There can never be an end until in some dim heaven of heavens sex ceases to be and duality ends its long war in unity."

Possibly the most beautiful and meaningful of these pictographs is that of a maiden with one foot resting upon a body of water wherein all is light and the other foot upon the sphere of earth which is veiled in darkness. In each hand she holds a cup, symbolic of the love and blessings she is pouring out upon the world. Above her head gleams an eight-pointed star, and within this star are two pyramids, one white and the other black. The latter is turned upside down, suggestive of disintegration and the transfer of its force to the white pyramid, luminous with eternal light. This maiden represents the spirit of the New Age which will usher in such wonder-working as is undreamed of at the present time.

Discovery of a New Planet

The discovery of a new planet will herald the advent of this New Age. Its orbit lies between those of Mercury and the Sun. As the unveilings of Pluto, Neptune and Uranus have worked so great a change in the life, manners and customs of this passing era, so the discovery of the new planet will bring about breath-taking wonders during the coming cycle. Man is already conquering time and space. Symbolic of this fact, beside the maiden is a plant bearing three full-blown blossoms while above it hovers a butterfly with out-spread wings. The latter signifies that in the glorious day ahead man's physical body will no longer be a prison-house for his spirit, but rather a vehicle which the spirit will be able to take up again at will in the course of its free exploration of the vast reaches of both heaven and earth.

Drama of Contrast

There is truly a wonderful mystery in black and white which touches upon the deepest secrets of the universe. Knowledge of this mystery will activate new levels of consciousness which will enable the awakened souls of tomorrow to become rovers among the stars. Ancient alchemists communicated many teachings relative to the contrasting forces of black and white and the results to be attained by their fusion. These teachings were usually given by means of allegories and parables.

This means of communicating the mystery involved is most graphically set forth in a medieval treatise published in 1542. It is titled *Solis Splendor*—the splendor of the Sun, or the Light of the World. To quote: "The Spirit dissolves the body, and in the dissolution extracts the soul of the body, and changes this body into soul, and the soul is changed into the Spirit, and the Spirit is again added to the body, for thus it has stability. Here then the body becomes spiritual by the strength of the Spirit. This the philosophers give to understand in the following signature, or figure. . . ."

Then follows the description of the picture of a *black* man standing half engulfed in the mire, representative of man's unredeemed personality. To his rescue comes a beautiful *white* maiden typifying the carnally transmuted nature into the purified body of light. Her radiant spirit-being is sometimes described in alchemical works as woman in liberation or as the feminine in exaltation. In *Solis Splendor* she is depicted "as adorned in a robe of many colors and with wings the feathers of which were like those of the finest white peacock, reflecting light like golden mirrors, and having quills adorned as with fine pearls."

"On her head," continues the description of this figure of light and beauty, "she had a crown of pure gold, and on top of it a silver star; around her neck she wore a necklace of fine gold, with the most precious ruby; her feet were clad with golden shoes, and the most beautiful fragrance emanated from her being. She clothed the man with a purple robe, lifted him up to his brightest clearness, and took him with herself to heaven. Therefore, says Senior, it is a living thing, which no more dies, but when used gives an eternal increase."

Students of Shakespeare who peer into the internal content of his immortal dramas soon come to recognize that they contain keys with which to unlock hidden mysteries of the spiritual life. An example of this is *Othello,* the story of a dark Moor and the exquisite white Desdemona. Had these two characters attained *polarity* within themselves, the tragedy they suffered could not have come to pass. And so we find that in this drama the Illumined Mind that inspired the Shakespearean works was communicating to all mankind the eternal truth of *polarity*.

In the Mystery Temples of old, aspirants entering the sacred initiatory precincts passed through a two-columned entrance. In some instances one of these columns was white, the other black, thus representing the two poles of spirit, the positive and the masculine and the feminine. In some cases the feminine column was broken or even in complete ruin, representative of the "fall," or the shattered polarity that occurred when infant humanity lost its unified Edenic state and entered upon the divided condition that followed, and under which humanity still lives.

Some pictorial representations of the Temple Entrance with one pillar broken show a woman weeping over the sorrow that all mankind has suffered in consequence of the broken law of polarity which it represents. In masonic symbology the broken pillar has been fittingly referred to as "the tomb of Hiram."

In the restored Mystery Temples of the dawning Aquarian Age there will be no broken column at their entrances. Both pillars will be whole and perfect, alike in size, proportion and color. There will be no weeping figure at the entrance. Again turning to masonic symbology, Hiram Abiff will not now be slain by the three ruffians of ignorance, superstition and fear. Equality between man and woman will have been so far restored through a balancing of the masculine and feminine principles that the two will enter the Temple of Light hand in hand, and in full realization of their perfect equality under the divine law of unity, or polarity.

PART III

NEW AGE DEVELOPMENTS

CHAPTER III

Color Therapy

The Spectrum and the Human Aura

he average student is familiar with the seven-tone diatonic scale and also with the twelve-tone chromatic scale in music. He is likewise familiar with the seven-tone color scale known as the spectrum. Few persons, however, know that as human sight becomes sensitized, and more refined instruments for investigation are developed, a twelve-tone color scale will be revealed. Those who possess ability to explore inner realms see therein many beautiful colors that are presently invisible to the average physical eye, some of them too exquisite for description.

Nevertheless, the power and magic of color are upon the threshold of far-reaching revelations. As New Age musicians are experimenting with a twelve-tone musical scale, so artists, attuned to New Age rhythms, will soon begin working with a twelve-hued spectrum. Professor Nicholas Roerich, possibly the foremost artist of our time by reason of his high spiritual attainment, employed, as only a master artist could, previously unknown astral colors in his magnificent creations. He set the impress of their luminosity upon his canvasses by using light in a way never before attempted. To quote his own words: "Color sounds the command of the future. Everything black, gray and misty has already sublimated the consciousness of humanity. One must again ponder about the gorgeous flower colors which always heralded the epochs of renaissance."

Perhaps the most deeply mystic definition of color is the one given by Goethe in these words: "Colors are the sufferings of light." As the vibratory rhythms of pure white light—which contains all colors within itself—is lowered, colors become manifest. Thus it is definitely a fact that colors are born through the sufferings of light.

There are three primary colors: blue, yellow and red. It is through blue that God the Father makes manifest the Will Principle, while the Christ manifests the Wisdom Principle through yellow. Red is the color whereby the Holy Spirit manifests the Activity Principle. Hence we have a Holy Trinity of color throughout the earth.

The secondary colors of the spectrum are orange, green, purple and indigo. Orange is a combination of red and yellow. Green is a combination of yellow and blue. Purple is a combination of red and blue. Indigo is a combination of orange, green blue and purple. A study of the various color combinations in relation to man's physical, mental, moral and spiritual development is a most fascinating subject.

Red

Reddish-brown indicates avarice, greed, selfishness.

Bright brick-red: anger.

Deep dark red: sensuality.

Scarlet reveals an over-abundance of personal pride.

Carmine—a clear pure red—denotes strength, endurance and a high state of physical perfection.

Clear, bright pink bespeaks human affection that has been softened by sorrow.

Orange

As previously noted, orange is a combination of red and yellow. The red typifies the personality; the yellow, the mentality.

Reddish or brick orange hues indicate that the forces of the personality control the mind.

Bright orange tones reveal what Christian Science practitioners would describe as the dominance of mind over matter.

All clear, golden-orange hues bespeak an awakening to the

values of true wisdom.

Yellow

Pure yellow indicates high intelligence and wisdom.

Luminous golden-yellow denotes adaptability for the reception and dissemination of wisdom.

Lemon-yellow gives evidence of a spiritualized or Christed mind.

Green

Green is the color which typifies balance and rest. In the spectrum it is the bridge, as it were, between personality as represented by red or orange and spirit as represented by blue or purple. Green is serene, restorative, healing. It is composed, as already stated, of yellow, the Christ color, and blue, the color assigned to God the Father.

That delicate silver-green seen in a forest after the first breath of spring is the life color. Could there be a more beautiful definition of life than to say that it is conceived by a blending of the Christ Wisdom with the Love of the Father?

Pale olive-green indicates sympathy and compassion.

Greenish-gray tones reveal pessimism as pale gray indicates fear.

Blue

Blue is in close attunement with the mystery of black. We think of it as a color that is nebulous or intangible. It is associated with wisps of blue smoke spiraling above chimney tops and bluish mists enfolding lofty mountain crests. It is through blue that we endeavor to penetrate the mysterious depths of the sea or the far reaches of the sky. So we say that God speaks to man of Infinity through the color blue.

Blue also connotes religious aspirations and devotion. If it has a faint touch of lavender, the devotion to a high and noble ideal.

Azure blue denotes a high phase of spirituality, a reaching toward the Infinite.

Blue-gray denotes religious feelings motivated by fear.

When the blue is mixed with dark reddish-brown, the religious tendencies are narrow and bigoted.

Purple

To repeat, purple is a combination of red and blue. In other words, it denotes purification and transmutation of the personality into spirituality. Since this path is also marked by sorrow, purple has long been associated with garments of mourning.

Clear, deep purple indicates spiritual power. For this reason purple robes have ever been associated with royalty, and the phrase "born to the purple" suggests majesty and kingly power.

Violet reveals a spiritualized nature, one made noble by sorrow. In many countries where it is the custom to wear black as a mark of grief over the passing of a loved one, violet is often called the color of "second mourning."

Lilac bespeaks of an out-reaching love for humanity.

Orchid is an Aquarian color which typifies the beautiful idealism belonging to the New Age. It will come into greater prominence as Aquarian idealism attains a wider expression in the life of mankind. In this connection it is significant to note that one of the newest developments in roses is an exquisite orchid tint.

Indigo

We, repeat, indigo is derived from a combination of orange, green, blue and purple.

The Indigo Ray is not yet well understood so is not in general use. Man is not fully aware of the power concentrated in the blending of the secondary colors. A greater use of the Indigo Ray belongs to some future day. *The Ray of synthesis.*

Black and White

Properly speaking, black is not a color. It is the absence of colors. While there is a tendency to associate black with evil, to the occult scientist it represents the negative or receptive condition upon which the positive powers of God work to bring latent being into external manifestation. Such is the statement in the opening chapter of Genesis: "In the beginning. . . the earth was without form, and void; and *darkness* was upon the face of the deep. And the Spirit of God moved upon the face of the waters."

This describes the fundamental nature of the creative process in its universal operations. Not until man becomes wise enough to rend the Veil of Isis will he be able to grasp something of the mystery here involved.

As all creation is inherent in God Himself, so does the great white light contain within itself all the colors of the spectrum. And it plays directly upon the divinity within man. As his latent divinity is awakened, he comes into attunement with the white light as a power.

God, the Father of our universe, manifests through the Blue Ray; hence blue is an infinite color. The Glorious One who manifests through the White Ray is beyond all planets, all stars, all constellations. Him we identify only as the Supreme Being.

Therapeutic Value of Colors

From the standpoint of their therapeutic value, the reds are stimulating and invigorating to man's physical body. The yellows vitalize and accelerate his mental activities. The greens are restful and soothing to his nervous system. The blues are inspirational, giving spiritual tone to his whole composition. The purples accelerate and sublimate all the processes of his body, mind and spirit. Each individual possesses his own spectrum, the color index of his character known as his aura.

A person of high idealism, whose thoughts, words and deeds are dedicated to the betterment of the world, will not have in his aura the murky reds of sensualism, the dull grays of fear and pessimism, or the dark muddy tones of hatred and malice. His aura will be luminous with bright, clear red, pure yellow, delicate blue, vibrant purple.

The human aura is an accurate index to character. Therein can be no subterfuge, no hypocrisy, no deception. The American sage, Ralph Waldo Emerson, once wrote something to this effect: I cannot hear what you say for what you *are* is shouting so loudly in my ears. In a study of the human aura we might well paraphrase this statement into "I cannot hear what you say because what I see in your aura proclaims so loudly what you really are."

Thus it is apparent that each experience and every event of a man's life is attuned to color. England's most exquisite poet, John Keats, wrote that life is a many-colored dome illuminated by the white light of Eternity.

We herewith append an excerpt from an old Rosicrucian book

and recommend it for study and meditation by every serious student. It will prove itself to be eminently worthwhile.

The Protective Aura

In all true occult schools students are taught a technique for creating and maintaining an aura of light as protection of body, mind and soul against all evil influences, whether directed consciously or unconsciously. This aura is an effective armor against all form of psychic attack and/or invasion. While the method is simple, it provides an effective and powerful means for warding off adverse psychic influences such as malicious mental magnetism, black magic and psychic vampirism, the latter being the drawing off of magnetic strength.

The method consists in forming a mental image of oneself surrounded by an aura of pure, clear, scintillant light. This image must be charged with a demand of the will that it serve the purpose for which it is being created. A little practice will enable one to' actually feel that in the presence and power of this white light is the radiation of Divine Spirit, the Spirit that is master of all things.

A teacher once said: "The highest and deepest occult teaching is that the white light must never be used for the purpose of an attack or personal gain, but may be properly employed by anyone at any time for self-protection against adverse psychic influences, whoever may exert them. It is a spiritual armor and may be employed in a constructive way whenever and wherever a need may arise."

Color Temples of the Future

It has often been stated in our writings that New Age religion will be centered in Initiation. Both color and music will play an important part in its work. There will be Color Temples wherein disciples and Initiates will be given more advanced teachings than the general public is ready to receive. The spiritual instruction of every civilization has contained meat for the strong, milk for babes.

These Color Temples will consist of seven structure keyed to the seven colors of the spectrum, and each building will be divided into seven compartments.

Color development has always been in harmony with human evolution. The most primitive of peoples had no color sense; they were aware of only black and white. It is said that in the time of Homer, about 900 B.C., humanity had become conscious of three colors: red, orange and yellow. Also in the Scandinavian epic, the Edda, the rainbow is referred to as having only three colors. Not until the Golden Age of Greece was lovely green light clearly perceived. The higher, more spiritual colors became visible at a much later date. This was not until man had developed certain spiritual faculties which enabled him to study spiritual laws.

Among the Color Temples of the future will be a Red Temple which will consist of seven compartments ranging from funda-mental tones of clear crimson to delicate shades of soft pink. Herein a disciple will learn how to transform *purity* into a power. We think of purity as a virtue, never as a power. Yet the Christ taught that only the pure in heart would have the ability to see God. It was said of Sir Galahad, the perfect Knight, that he had the power of ten because his heart was pure.

In the Orange Temple will be waged the battle between personality (red) and wisdom (yellow). This will be the arena of the Great Overcoming. In a compartment of luminous orange-gold or gold-orange a disciple will eventually comprehend the significance of words uttered by Solomon, the great wisdom king: "He that is slow to anger is better than the mighty; and he that ruleth his spirit than he that taketh a city."

Yellow Temple work will be devoted largely to development of the mind. In the pure glory of its highest compartment a disciple will learn the full meaning of illuminating or Christing the mind, and will then comprehend the significance of St. Paul's instruction to his disciples: "Let this mind be in you, which was also in Christ Jesus."

Both disciples and Initiates will study the wonders of life in the Green Temple, where they will learn to extract certain life forces from nature and will be taught to pass these life forces into human bodies by way of the spleen for the purpose of rejuvenating and regenerating them. Thus they will be able to overcome the diseases and crystallization now looked upon as the ravages of old age. Amid the glory of the silver-green light which suffuses the highest compartment of this Temple, an Initiate will stand before the very mystery of life itself and there comprehend the deep significance of the Master's words: "I am come that they might have life, and have it more abundantly."

Workings of spiritual law will be studied in the Blue Temple. The operations of this law are today considered as miracles. Bathed in the exquisite azure tones of the highest compartment of the Blue Temple, Illumined Ones will study the operation of this law in the highest realms to which the earth planet is attuned.

We have previously stated in this series that the full power of the Indigo Ray has not been manifested as yet. In the Color Temples of the New Age, however, this Ray will come into full functioning. Thereby Initiates will travel at will through cosmic space to contact and commune with dwellers on other planets. Then Saturn will no longer be considered the planet of obstruction as it is today, but will be looked upon as the pathfinder and wayshower for the Illumined.

Spiritual law governing the higher realms will continue to be studied in the Purple Temple, but now this law will be brought down and manifested on the earth plane. Sensitized by the exquisite Orchid Ray of its higher compartments, man will become a self-conscious citizen of two worlds. He will be able to pass at will from earth to heaven and to answer calls for service in any realm where it is needed. He will then join with St. Paul and other emancipated souls in the triumphant song, "O death, where is thy sting? O grave, where is thy victory?"

In this study of Color Temples of the future we have purposely illustrated the various steps by means of quotations from the Bible because we desired to demonstrate how truly the Bible is the supreme Mystery Book of Life.

So often one hears students of advanced thought remark, "I left the Bible behind when I left the Orthodox Church. Now that I'm a student of occult or higher thought, I have outgrown the Bible." Such a statement evidences a complete misunderstanding of the purpose and message of the Bible. One can never outgrow this Wonder Book. The further one goes in spiritual unfoldment, the more the Bible will reveal its marvelous spiritual treasures.

For man, the Bible will be the supreme textbook of life to the very end of his evolution on this planet. Not until the conclusion of this great incarnational cycle will he fully comprehend the meaning of the biblical promise, "Ye shall know the truth, and the truth shall make you free."

CHAPTER IV

Cosmic Aspects of Color

Living Energies in Color Rays

he occult scientist does not look upon light and its colors as mere lifeless forces of nature; nor indeed does he look upon nature as being lifeless. The universe, or cosmos, is to him a living organism permeated throughout, in every least particle, by the Supreme Intelligence which we call God.

Just as there is a spirit "behind" or "within" the human body, so there is a spirit behind or within the physical orb of the Sun; and that spiritual Sun is invisible to the physical eye just as the human spirit is invisible to it.

When the esotericist speaks of the Cosmic Christ it is this invisible, interior, spiritual Sun to which he refers, and it is this Cosmic Christ of the Sun which he calls the Savior not only of the planet earth but of all the planetary bodies of our solar system: Mercury, Venus, Mars, Jupiter, Saturn, together with their satellites.

The relationship of the Cosmic Christ with the outer planets, Uranus, Neptune, Pluto, and trans-Plutonian planets, is one of the deep mysteries of our solar evolution. From the human point of view it must of course be said that the Cosmic Christ works with these planets also, but it must be added that the nature of the work is very different from that done with earth humanity.

The white light that comes from our Sun is actually not a pure white light. Our Sun is a yellow, or yellow-orange, star, and even sunlight is tinged with its gold color, which in esotericism is the Christ color. It is significant that the bands of color in the aura of Christ Jesus is also said, by those who have seen them, to lie in the same arrangement of bands as the colors of our solar spectrum, whereas those of the aura of Gautama Buddha, for example, differ. Astronomers know that different stars have different spectra, and the esotericist follows this up with the statement that every human individual also has a distinctive spectrum of auric or spirit colors, arranged in characteristic bands.

An ordinary human being has an aura in which the bands of color lie across, or through, the ovoid aura of radiation which surrounds his body; each band is incomplete. In the divine aura of cosmic Beings and Adepts the auric bands extend in a complete circle and their arrangement shows what type of evolution the Being represents, just as the spectrum of the star reveals to the astronomer what type of star he is dealing with. That there is a true correlation between the spectra of the stars and nebulae and those of the auras of cosmic Beings is the contention of the occult scientist, but this is an aspect of auric science which has yet to be developed in the New Age.

We have shown previously that the three primary colors of the solar spectrum as related to our evolutionary scheme also indicate the three primary cosmic forces of the Solar Logos, which in Christian terminology, are correlated with the Trinity: Father, Son and Holy Spirit. The Blue Ray belongs to the Father Principle, the Yellow Ray to the Christ Principle and the Red Ray to the Holy Spirit. In its physical manifestation the material universe is on the Red Ray.

The Virgin Spirit—humanity in its pure essence—is also a trinity of powers, which in Rosicrucian terminology are designated as the Divine Spirit, the Life Spirit and the Human Spirit. Each power possesses a correlative "sheath" or vehicle. In the Eastern philosophy these are called Atma, Buddhi and Manas. The sheath of the latter is the casual body or, in Rosicrucian terminology, the Human Spirit.

When the Virgin Spirit becomes indwelling in a body organism, the three Rays or powers have special centers through which they work. The Divine Spirit (Will Principle, correlating to the Father), has its seat at the root of the nose, between the eyes. The Blue Ray of the Solar Logos impinges upon this center in working upon human consciousness. This Ray is concerned entirely with the well-being of the spiritual man. It is a dissolving Ray and burns up all useless conditions in the universe. It is called the Father Fire.

Forces emanating from the Christ Principle, or Cosmic Christ (the Love-Wisdom Principle), aid the evolutionary development of the life on each one of the planets of the solar system, and when that life has reached a certain stage it is said that the Cosmic Christ becomes *indwelling.* This is the point at which involution becomes evolution, when the evolving life, having reached the nadir of its involvement in matter, turns Godward, to evolve upward out of materiality and into the contemplation of spirit.

The Christ Ray is yellow or golden, and is nourishing and upbuilding in nature. It is concerned chiefly with man's mental and moral development. It is transmitted through the planets which reflect to the earth influences consonant with their own evolutionary status, working chiefly on the brain and through the ductless glands in the human organism.

Those forces which reach us by way of the Moon, which are also reflections of solar light, represent the Red Ray of the Holy Spirit or Jehovistic Principle, and they enter the body through the spleen, their chief function having to do with the well-being of the physical man.

When the esotericist speaks of God as *Light,* and describes Him in terms of color, it must be remembered that the "Rays" of that light are in fact living Beings. Thus Hebrew legend has it that thousands of new souls are created daily before the Throne of God, welling up like a fountain of light and flowing out into the universe. So also it is to be understood that the "Rays" of the Cosmic Christ represent a life wave of Archangels, and that the particular Being whom we call The Christ, and who worked through the agency of the Master Jesus, was the greatest of these Rays or Archangels—an individualized Being who came to earth at the beginning of our Christian era, at which time earth's evolution was given the necessary redemptive impulse to counteract the death-dealing influences that had entered our earthly sphere at the time of the "fall." A similar occurrence awaits some planets of our system, and has already been known on others. Thus we see that the threefold power is active in many and varied spheres, and it operates in manifold ways.

We have said that the outer planets have a special relationship to the Cosmic Christ and His work with earth humanity. This work concerns the awakening of the two centers of psychic power in the head, the pineal gland and pituitary body. The awakening of these two centers will be the signature of the coming race, for it will be the common heritage of all and not just the rare development of the few that it is today.

The Spiritual Head Centers

The pituitary body transmits the Rays of Uranus which open the etheric doors between heaven and earth and demonstrate beyond any doubt that there is no death. The pineal gland transmits the Rays of Neptune which enable the illumined one to enter directly into heavenly realms and to study at first hand the laws and so-called miracles of the higher planes. At the present time it is exceedingly difficult to stir these psychic sense centers from their dormant condition, and the exercises given in the Mystery Schools to accomplish this are fraught with danger. But it will be one of the great blessings of the New Age that the awakening will be accomplished without danger through the use of color therapy in the Color Temples which we have already described, for color can be administered in such wise as to safely kindle these sleeping organs of the soul into intense activity.

It is to be understood that the real stimulating force in every instance is the triune Virgin Spirit itself, responding to the cosmic powers of the Logos; but in the dense materialistic conditions of the earth plane certain outside helps are provided by the Lords of Destiny, who see to it that each cycle has what is needed for its unfoldment at any given time. Thus the cosmic Rays, which science says are increasing in the earth's atmosphere, are among such helps provided by the Lords of Destiny.

The accelerated vibrations necessary to awaken the power centers in the head from latency to activity will, in many instances, be accomplished through color stimulation, thereby causing those in whom they are awakened to become, here and now, citizens of two worlds—"rovers amid the stars," as such attainment was designated by the Sons of Wisdom in ancient Egypt.

Writes Dr. Minugh in an article on color that appeared in the magazine *Chimes:*

> In the Golden Age of Greece, and in the Healing Temples of Light and Color at Heliopolis in ancient Egypt, color was used effectively, and was greatly revered. Throughout all the ages there has always been the application of color to establish poise and harmony, to soothe and sustain, to heal and restore, and to create anew. . .
>
> Color application has the beautiful and purposeful mission of alleviating dis-ease, not with drugs, but with the radiant pristine *Power of Light* which works on *all levels* of our *Being.* It is due to an inability to illumine our lives emotionally, mentally, and spiritually that we suffer loss of tone and dis-ease physically. . .
>
> We have seen major glandular centers in the human body. . . These centers each have their own particular rate of vibration (color frequency) and absorb from the food we eat, the thoughts we think, the emotions we harbor, certain qualities whose rate of frequency is identical respectively with each of the seven colors of the spectrum.
>
> The white light (Christ-light) drawn into the consciousness of the soul is changed into its seven component colors, each one being sent to sustain the center to which it has its affinity. . .

New devices for transcribing inspirational sound-patterns into gorgeous color symphonies will undoubtedly revolutionize man's color consciousness and aid in the development of his inner plane awareness. This will greatly enhance the quality and productiveness of all the creative arts. Fourth dimensional activities will come noticeably to the fore in science, art, literature and religion. Humanity stands upon the threshold of a *color-full* world, one that will challenge it to delve into the unknown, the undiscovered, the unlimited.

Scientific Application of Color

Advanced cases of psychoneurosis, obsession, and shell-shock will be soothed by the violet-lavender Ray of Neptune, the most healing of all colors.

For extreme cases of nervous exhaustion, hypersensitiveness, morbidity and undue introspection and brooding, the inspiring blue-gold of Uranus will be found especially beneficial.

Fevers, high blood pressure and heart palpitation will respond to the soothing effect of Mercury's pure green-gold.

Low blood pressure, anemia and general lack of physical stamina will require the clear, exhilarating red of Mars.

Tendencies toward excitability resulting from an over-abundance of nervous energy will be lessened by using the indigo ray of Saturn. Bone fractures and malconstruction will respond to this ray also.

Ailments centering in the liver and impediment of the arterial circulatory system will be aided by the use of Jupiter's deep violet-purple.

Skin diseases, irregularities in the venous circulatory system, melancholia and ordinary ailments common to childhood, will be benefited by the soft pink and gold belonging to the love star Venus.

Heart ailments of all kinds, from slight irregularity in beat caused by nervous indigestion to the most serious affliction, will respond favorably to the magical properties of the pure deep golden ray of the Sun, the heart of the solar system to which we belong.

Students of the occult arts, and all who are mystically inclined, when utilizing any of the fine arts as a medium through which to promulgate these higher principles governing life, will find it helpful to draw upon the exquisite blue-lavender tints belonging to Neptune. Writers and speakers whose messages are centered in New Age ideals of unity, cooperation and brotherhood will find their inspiration quickened by using the blue and gold of Uranus.

Teachers, scientists, physicians, nurses and metaphysical healers will be strengthened in their respective professions by the soft, clear greens and gold of Mercury.

Dieticians, naturopaths, chiropractors, osteopaths and other healers using natural methods of correction and restoration, will be definitely helped in their ministrations by centering their remedial activities in the orange-gold of the Sun augmented by the clear greens of Mercury.

Ministers, lawyers, public speakers and politicians will enhance their influence by use of the pure violet-purple of Jupiter. Athletes, soldiers, farmers, and all outdoor workers will increase both energy and endurance by using the vibrant reds of Mars.

The Moon governs prenatal growth and the early years of infancy. Its soft mist-like green and silver tones are indicated for the ills of infants and for women during the months of prospective motherhood. Mothers, teachers of very young children, matrons of orphanages, and all who have the care and direction of little ones will be greatly aided and stimulated in their work by the lovely pink-gold tones of Venus.

Spirit, mind and body—man in the whole of his being—are attuned to the heavenly spheres. Disease could never touch that wholeness or disturb its harmony had he always lived true to cosmic law.

Zodiacal Influences

Alan Leo, the English astrologer, once said that the zodiac is the alphabet from which astrologers obtain words of power for interpreting heavenly symbolism. It is, he adds, a circle of mystery more profound than the planets. This being true, the brief synopsis of color therapeutics herein outlined must necessarily include something of zodiacal as well as of planetary color patterns.

Emanations of the twelve zodiacal Hierarchies play upon the body of man, each having its own psychic entrance gate. Thus, from Aries, governing the head, to Pisces, governing the feet, the human organism is a sounding board whereby every zodiacal body emits its own particular keynote, and rays forth its own distinctive color and color pattern. Hence it is that the human body-temple is a perfect reflection of the heavenly pattern as shown in the arrangement of planets and signs in the horoscope. The star-patterns at birth are a complete index to the evolution of the ego coming into incarnation, and to the type of body prepared for meeting its earthly requirements.

Again, in conformity with the starry pattern above in which the twelve signs are divided into quaternaries corresponding to the four basic elements—Fire, Air, Earth and Water—are the four "vehicles" man uses in his progressive evolution. The Fire signs (Aries, Leo and Sagittarius) represent the pure flame of spirit; the Air signs (Gemini, Libra and Aquarius), the powers of mind; the Water signs (Cancer, Scorpio and Pisces), the emotional nature; and the Earth signs (Taurus, Virgo and Capricorn), relate to the physical body-temple.

As previously noted, each of the twelve signs emits its own individual sound and radiates its own individual color. Each keynote has its seven octaves and each color possesses its seven varying tints. Some of these colors are too delicate to be seen by the physical eye, but their effect upon man's body and consciousness are beginning to be tabulated by those experimenting in color psychology and color therapeutics.

One of the most important phases of healing through color and sound is the awakening realization of the healer to the fact that both thinking and feelings are intimately connected with physical ills, and that in them lie the cause as well as the cure of disease.

The fundamental color emanation of Aries, the first zodiacal sign, is red; Taurus, yellow-pink; Gemini, deep violet; Cancer, green-silver; Leo, orange-gold; Virgo, clear violet; Libra, yellow; Scorpio, red; Sagittarius, purple-blue; Capricorn, indigo; Aquarius, indigo in lighter hues; Pisces, blue.

It will be understood that each fundamental color has its seven-fold aspect that blends or unites it with each of the other six colors in the New Age science of color therapy and color psychology. Much additional experimentation and observation will be required in order to determine the varying effects of the many possible color combinations.

We have noted that the twelve signs of the zodiac are divided into four triplicities correlating to the four basic elements in nature, and that these same divisions correlate to man's lower quaternary—the threefold body together with mind—which constitutes the composite vehicle wherein an ego functions on earth. The same classification pertains to diseases, all of which fall into one or another of these four groupings. To illustrate: infirmities caused by alcoholic excesses, fevers, high blood pressure, and that most dreaded disease of all human scourges, cancer, all come under the element Fire. All forms of insanity and drug excesses relate to the Air element. Diseases of the stomach, digestive tract, assimilative and glandular systems come under the Water element. Abnormal growths and malformations of the body belong to the element Earth.

A healer will do his most successful work when dealing with ailments that come under the same element as his ruling sign. For example, a physician whose birth month is Leo (July 20-August 20, approximately) will have special ability for healing maladies classifying under the Fire element or its complement, Air, because naturally he will have greater affinity with patients who belong to Fire or Air.

Most healers, regardless of the school they represent and whether or not the astrological factors are recognized, admit that they are more successful in dealing with some diseases than with others. The key to this fact is to be found in the element which links the healer and the patient, together with the nature of the ailment to be cured. These are the bases of specialization as yet unknown to physicians.

The twelve zodiacal signs bestow vitality of varying degrees as well as different characteristics, temperaments and personal appearances. They are truly sign posts of life. The response or affinity of any individual to the various degrees of sound and color as emanated by the birth sign, indicates the native's evolutionary status. This also aids in the person's adaptability and susceptibility to healing through music and color.

Below is a brief tabulation of the general maladies coming under each of the twelve signs:

ARIES: Ailments affecting the cerebral hemisphere of the brain, organs of the head, eyes and ears.

TAURUS: Neck, throat, larynx, tonsils, carotid arteries and jugular veins.

GEMINI: Shoulders, arms, lungs, thymus and upper ribs.

CANCER: Stomach, diaphragm, lacteas and thorasic duct.

LEO: Heart, spinal cord and aorta.

VIRGO: Large and small intestines and pancreas.

LIBRA: Kidneys, skin and the suprarenals.

SCORPIO: Bladder, urethra, the genital organs, rectum and descending colon.

SAGITTARIUS: Hips, thighs, femur, illium, illiac arteries and veins and sacral region (lower part of spine).

CAPRICORN: Knees, bones (in general) and certain skin eruptions.

AQUARIUS: Limbs from knees to ankles and varicose veins.

PISCES: Maladies principally of the feet and toes.

It should be noted that indispositions coming under a certain sign may have a reflex in its opposite or complementary sign. This important factor must not be overlooked in making a general diagnosis.

To recapitulate briefly, a complete delineation of a person's condition of health or disease requires a proper examination of all the numerous factors involved in his composite being. This means taking into account the Sun's rulership over the indwelling ego; Mercury's over its mind; Venus over its emotions; the Moon over its instincts; Mars over its drives; Jupiter over its etheric and physical bodies; Saturn as its stabilizer and chastener—the ego's supreme teacher. Through pain and sorrow he tends to lift the ego above the trivial and evanescent and to focus its attention upon spirit and eternal truths. Thus it is that regeneration and illumination so often follow upon sickness and grief.

As the world moves closer to the cooperative new age of Aquarius, healing groups will be established to work along specialized lines in correlation with the cosmic scheme of the twelve signs and the seven planets.

CHAPTER V

The Psychology of Color in Everyday Living

Color in Dress and the Home

y the ordering of Divine Wisdom Nature surrounds mankind with an infinite variety of colors, a wonderful fact which is all too often taken for granted. Natures's wealth of colorings is as much the result of intelligent design as the colors on a canvas. They have not, however, always been as rich and meaningful as they are today. Evolution pertains to the whole of nature, and this includes her color scheme which has undergone many changes since the first dawn of life on this planet.

Only as man becomes cognizant of the psychology of color does he begin to realize the divine beneficence that adapts natural hues to his status in time, place and circumstance. Mankind itself is an integral part of the grand scheme of nature; he is not a thing apart, and he intuitively takes to himself that which Nature abundantly provides. The trends in color as used in daily life seem on the surface to be trivial; in actuality they have their roots deep in the human psyche.

Every woman has an affinity for certain colors. These are the colors with which she should surround herself, not only by using them in her wearing apparel but in the decoration of her home; and, if possible, her office or place of work.

It is well to experiment with colors until finding the one which is most congenial. As we ascend the ladder of spiritual attainment mentally, morally and physically, we find that we are also ascending in the degree of sensitivity to color and light. The writer once knew a young woman who was quite physical in her outlook on life. She dressed largely in red and had her apartment done in clear bright crimson. Later she became a student of philosophy, spending most of her day in the libraries of the city in which she lived. She knew nothing of the psychology of color at that time but intuitively she changed the decoration of her home to soft golden and bright yellows. Still later she became a metaphysical student and changed her colors to the softest azure blues. In her final years she was a profound student of the occult, and wrote much on super-physical verities. Then it was that she lived, moved and had her being solely in the delicate, almost tenuous, New Age tones of orchid. So beautiful and so ... as the atmosphere of her apartment that one could almost hear the music of her angelic companions.

As people come to realize more and more the importance of surrounding themselves with the psychologically right colors, interior decoration has become a most popular profession for both men and women. For example, a decorator will take a room having a northern exposure, and instead of white or gray walls that present a cold and cheerless appearance in a north light, he will have the walls done in pale, sunshiny yellow. The light from a blazing fire in an open fireplace will give the room such a charming, cozy atmosphere that the lack of direct sunlight will be scarcely perceptible.

A nervous person or one suffering from insomnia will get much benefit from having the room occupied done in the soft green tones of the forest in early spring. A lonely, solitary person, one who does not make friends easily and who fails to attract companionship, will be benefited by surroundings done in shades of pink, ranging from bright tones to palest peach-blossom tints. For a person engaged in creative work, or for a metaphysical student who spends much time in prayer and meditation, the softest azure blue, a color which seems to hold within itself the key to infinity, is recommended.

Color in New Age Education

Since the close of World War II each year has shown an increasing interest in color experimentation in the various schools, both public and private. In some of our American cities, schools have been built according to specifications jointly prepared by architects, educators and psychologists. The latter specialists saw to it that color and light were properly incorporated into the structures. The blackboards were green, the chalk yellow, the walls in three delicate tints. Children's lunches were served in plastic dishes of many hues. Light streams into the rooms through walls and ceilings constructed largely of glass brick. So it is that beauty and brightness are coming with the dawning of a truly new day. During the next few decades, as man comes to a greater realization of the potency of color in human affairs, it is certain to be used more and more in the classroom.

The color motif will follow the pattern of the solar spectrum, but with the addition of peach-blossom, purple, black and white. In the early grades instruction will be given in rooms of bright, clear scarlet. As the mental faculties of the children are awakened and stimulated, the intermediate grades will be taught in rooms of clear bright yellows and greens. When the students are ready for scientific and abstract studies, these will be taught in rooms decorated in various shades of blue, indigo and purple. By this time studies in extra-sensory perception will have become an essential part of the regular school curriculum. Those students who are ready to study such subjects as the development of telepathy, clairvoyance, clair-audience and kindred subjects will receive instruction in rooms of softest mauve and all the exquisite orchid shades.

Intimations of such interesting and far-reaching innovations have echoed and re-echoed down through the ages. An eleventh century poet sings:

Sun Cloud and Rain beget the Bow
What moral is here calling?

Color in Industry

The effect of color on people, animals and units in the vegetable kingdom will be studies and the result of these studies will be the development of etheric vision, or the power to see the next grade of matter with the physical eye. Increasingly will people think and talk in terms of light. . . —Alice A. Bailey.

Colors are being used in factories for their psychological effect on the workers. Brighter surroundings, it has been found, mean a higher output of first-class work and fewer accidents. A bad case of the "blues" is often due to an overdose of depressing grays or browns in the surroundings.

In one factory near London, absenteeism among women employees soared to an alarming rate. A color specialist who was called in noticed that the lighting made the women's faces look a sickly blue. One glance in the mirror, and they felt ill. A coat of warm beige over the iron gray walls neutralized this effect, and the absentee problem was solved.

The brilliant colors favored by South Americans stand in sharp contrast to the more subdued hues generally adopted by North Americans. Psychologists have recognized the business potentialities of this fact. For example, three large American firms were competing for a South American half-million-dollar order for electric irons. One of the firms cleverly substituted bright crimson for the usual black on the handles of the irons and secured the order.

Color becomes increasingly important in the daily life of all peoples. Everyone responds to the soul's craving for color and light which lift above the darker shades of materialism.

Illustrative of industry's increasing awareness of the power and efficacy of color are the following interesting excerpts from *Popular Science Monthly:*

Girls in an air-conditioned mid-western factory complained of feeling cold, although the temperature was kept at a steady 72. When the blue-green walls were repainted a warm coral color, however, their complaints ceased. In another plant, workers lifting black metal boxes filled with briar pipes complained that they strained their backs. One weekend the foreman had the boxes painted pale green. On Monday morning several men commented, "Say, these new light-weight boxes make a real difference."

Such evidences of the deceptive and persuasive powers of color are not new to science. The average person will underestimate the temperature of a blue room and overestimate the temperature of a red one, and will judge dark-colored objects to be heavier than they really are. In the last ten years the science of color engineering has put these and other color phenomena to practical work on a broad scale.

While red impels to action, green—the color of nature—seems to promote a sense of well-being. Blackfriars Bridge in London was notorious for suicides. When its black ironwork was repainted bright green, suicides from the bridge declined by more than one third.

Shipowners stand to save millions of dollars because of the discovery by the Scripps Institution of Oceanography that barnacles, the marine organisms that foul ships by attaching themselves to hulls, are particularly fond of dark colors and will settle in far fewer numbers on light green or white. A simple way, surely to decrease American shipping's $100,000,000 annual "barnacle bill."

Wartime experience developed a complete color program for industry, with results so impressive that hundreds of factories are adopting it. Managers attribute production increases of 15 to 30 percent solely to scientific selection of colors.

Color Prognostication

Mass consciousness expresses its prevailing color awareness in dress, lighting, decorations and other media. And events, too, have their inherent color elements. When these are of a universal character and charged with deep significance, they quickly translate themselves through human consciousness into corresponding colors on the plane of expression. Constant talk of war during 1939, and its actual outbreak prior to the end of that year, made red the predominant fashion in wearing apparel. As the war spread in 1940, red gained in popularity. Hats, dresses, coats and handbags of scarlet were conspicuous in any large assemblage.

This was in keeping with nature's requirement, for bright red is the color related to strength, courage, initiative and physical activity. It is valor's own radiation, a quality needed for the successful prosecution of the conflict.

Red is a martial color. When the god of war hovers over a nation, he waves a red flag. When thought forms of war envelop a people, its psychological reaction manifests as a predominance of scarlet in the world of fashion.

As the war progressed, something more was needed. The stress and strain of 1942 and 1943 was tending to break down man's fighting spirit. Morale builders became another need. Here again color played an indispensible role. The brightest hues imaginable came to the fore, the more glaring and vivid the better. So there followed a season of royal purples, brilliant fuchsias and rich magentas, often used together in the most striking combinations. Some were fairly breathtaking and they served to give vibrancy to the human spirit, lifting it above doubt and sorrow, depression and despair. They had the effect of turning the mind's eye toward the cloud's silver lining. All this was indicative of the brighter days on the other side of the trial.

The year 1944 was a pastel year. The brilliant and climactic combinations of color were succeeded by exquisitely soft and soothing tints. A need for their healing effect had come. After long-drawn-out months of war, the suspense and agony of waiting for news, the heartbreak evidenced by the too frequent display of a golden star, people could no longer tolerate the galvanic effect of vivid colors. Victory on the battlefront was already conceded, its fulfillment only a matter of time. Hence, rather than a continued incitement to action, an attitude of poise was essential for concluding the conflict and making peace. This poise was the message that pastels introduced into that important work.

The pastel tints found beautiful expression in the Christmastide decorations of 1944. In some of our most famous big-city department stores, the decorative motifs for both window display and interiors were not in the conventional reds and greens so much as in delicate rainbow colorings. In keeping with this trend, there was at least one important instance where the traditional Santa

Claus was replaced by silver-misted angels. Commenting on the change, the manager of one such emporium expressed the hope that this innovation in its color scheme would lessen in Christmas shoppers the stress and strain of nerve tension.

With the conclusion of the war in 1945 thoughts were being directed toward healing the cleavages it had brought and effecting larger unities among people and nations. One World became almost a slogan of the time. So while the need for the solace and healing of pastels was still present and remained in the forefront of fashion, the color that then came to prevail was a lovely blue, the blue described as dusty or ash blue. This is the soft, misty shade of a June sky, the color that belongs to healing, idealism, aspiration and dreams of a better day in a better world.

It might be said that 1946 saw the birth of a new world, for the atomic bomb had sounded the death of the old one. The thought uppermost in many minds and the word on thousands of lips was that we had come to a turning point where the choice was between one world or none. Mass consciousness was concerned as never before with international relationships. And once again the trend in men's thinking was reflected in the prevailing modes. We quote from a fashion note of that day: "The spring prints all tell their own story. There are Gulliver's Travels, and Chinese influence was strongly marked. One designer featured a Chinese blouse with Russian decorations, to be worn with a Spanish sash—another evidence that we dress as we feel and think."

As we have said, red was the dominant color during the first years of the war, the red of destruction. But red is also the color of initiative and action, so for building a new world red still had work to do and was much in evidence. Now, however, it appeared in a combination appropriate to its constructive role. Golden yellow is the unifying color, and binder. A fashion note of that period states that golden red (tomato) was being shown extensively and bade fair to become extremely popular. The influence of the yellow as fused with the red was reflected in the efforts to establish the United Nations as a successfully functioning organization, another evidence of the color forces that are at work beneath the surface becoming outwardly manifest in our everyday environment.

It is now for the gold in the heart of mankind to transmute the red of war and conquest into the golden red of the day star that humanity may "walk in the light, as he is in the light" and so have true and lasting fellowship, one with another.

In an article which appeared in the *New Age Interpreter* for October 1949, it was observed that the latest fashion notes listed red as the most popular color. Smartly dressed women were wearing complete ensembles in red—hat, dress coat, purse and shoes. Navy blue, black and brown, previously so widely favored for winter wear, were being replaced by the Martian color. It was then recalled that the last time red was fashion's decree was the winter of 1940 and 1941; and that, true to its signification, it heralded our entry into World War II immediately following Japan's attack upon Pearl Harbor. Then it was asked if a return to red in women's fashions presaged events of a like nature, or if it was merely a carry-over from the sanguinary years so recently brought to a close. "Time will tell" was the article's conclusion.

And so it did. In 1950 the United States engaged in another blood-letting struggle in Korea. Colors certainly speak a prophetic language if we would but interpret them right.

In these days of extreme peril and stress, if suddenly fashion should decree that brilliant crimson was to be the predominating color note of the coming season, in the light of past color prognostications we might well surmise that the war god is hovering very near.

Color Meditation

Until the time comes when some New Age inventor brings to earth a true color-organ, aspirants will find it necessary to do their own work of experimentation, following in the steps of the musician or clairvoyant who can lay down a few simple, basic rules. We have shown in another place the correlations of the color schemes with activities of various kinds. There remains to give a simple technique for making direct personal use of color, which can be combined with music as the student himself chooses.

It is always possible to purchase color lamps in whatever color one desires to use. However, Truth students who are learning to understand something of the wonderful powers of concentration and visualization are beginning creatively by taking daily "color baths" in meditation; for physical colors are the merest shadow of the vital, powerful color formations of the spiritual world.

The colors most conducive to spiritual meditation are in the violet and amethsyt range, and also blue-violet and the deep dark blue of indigo—these colors corresponding to the spiritual force-centers of the head. Leonardo da Vinci said that the power of meditation was increased tenfold if the meditation were done under the rays of violet light falling through stained glass windows of a quiet church.

Blue is a color which is soothing and quieting, and therefore exceptionally good for meditation, especially on spiritual and altruistic subjects. It induces a tranquillity of mind which is highly receptive to spiritual inspiration. It is especially the color of the devotional mood and stimulates the desire for devotional exercises. It is the color of the Madonna.

In the work of meditation, the surroundings should be as quiet as conditions will permit, and always, if possible, there should be the background of soothing and restful music. One should assume a completely relaxed posture, either reclining on a couch or seated in a comfortable chair. After the body tensions are relaxed one should visualize the color appropriate to the theme chosen for meditation, and imagine it in soft oncoming rhythms like the waves of the sea. First the waves cover the feet, then rise to the knees, then to the waist, to the heart, to the throat; and finally they cover the head. So one laves and bathes in this harmony of color for ten, fifteen, twenty, or even thirty minutes at a time, completely shutting out the world, and living in a veritable sea of color. The effect is stimulating and renewing.

Until one becomes thoroughly familiar with the art of color bathing it is best to keep the mind entirely quiescent. However, after becoming at ease with the process it will help to meditate upon some favorite inspirational poem, or a well-loved passage of Scripture, such as, "Be still and know that I am God;" "He leadeth me beside the still waters;" "Surely goodness and mercy shall follow me all the days of my life and I shall dwell in the house of the Lord forever."

This method of color meditation is applicable to the healing of others as well as oneself. It can be used in spiritual healing clinics in which each of the twelve signs and nine planets (and the satellite Moon) is represented by a healer who works for patients whose horoscopes are harmonious with his own. Such healing groups will become focal centers for an inflow of tremendous spiritual power; a power so vast, a spirit so mighty, that those who come to scoff will remain to praise, and mayhap even to pray!

CHAPTER VI

Color and Music in the New Age

Color Vision

 o the esotericist, color vision means that the spiritual eye of clairvoyance has become aware of the living colors which are a basic phenomenon of the soul world. On the astral plane—also called the Desire World because it is the realm of nature in which emotions, feelings and desires are visible in objective formations—clouds of color display the qualities of the soul life of the entire human race. Here also are seen the color formations created by the cosmic emotions of Angels and Archangels, and other cosmic Beings; as well as by animals and those nature spirits which work in the plant and mineral kingdoms.

At a deeper or higher stratum of the soul world the basic quality is *sound*, for this is the realm of the *Music of the Spheres* and here the archetypal songs of creation resound through space. The two realms, called the First and Second Heavens in Western Wisdom tradition, are not separated from one another. Rather, they interpenetrate; and the color-patterns seen in the soul world are, in fact, "ensouled" by the harmonies of the next higher or inner plane.

Where thoughts and emotions are intricate and highly civilized, the sound and color-patterns are correspondingly intricate. These patterns in the astral vary from mere puffs of color like small clouds, which in the aggregate resemble rolling cloud masses to

68

clouds of collective emotions that ofttimes surge and roll over vast multitudes of people. It is within such masses that the great Archangels who guide the evolution of races and nations may sometimes be seen directing their charges—as many seers have described them in sacred literature the world over.

The stirring martial music of patriotic songs sends armies into battle in a wave of scarlet, crimson and gold combined with flashing, shifting blades of light representing righteous indignation and a strong spirit of self-defense. It is not surprising that these blades of light in the aura are mistaken for actual spears and swords in the hands of supernatural warriors; although in general the blades surround their bodies in a sort of aureole. Such is the representation of high moral courage, but not the excitement of anger shown in lightning-like formations of the aura against a black-and-scarlet background.

Where the thought processes are clearly defined, as they are in a trained intellect, the thought forms are sharp and clear. The human aura also reveals this line of development, it being cloudy and indefinite of outline in those of the masses; clear of outline, radiantly transparent and brilliant with living color in those of higher culture.

In an unsigned article which appeared in *Rays from the Rose Cross Magazine* for October 1915 and presumably written by Max Heindel, who was then its editor, we read: "When we learn to control our sense of sight so that we may look at a man without seeing his physical form, then his photo-sphere or aura may be seen in all its splendor, for the colors of earth are dull in comparison with those spiritual living fires which surround and emanate from each human being. The fantastic coruscating play of the aurora-borealis gives us an idea of how this photo-sphere or shadow acts; it is in incessant motion, darts of force and flame are constantly shooting out from every part thereof, but particularly active around the head; and the colors and hues of this auric atmosphere change with every thought or move."

Tonal Equivalents of Form and Color
The thought form proper, which has to do with ideas not

associated with a feeling or emotion, also shows that a correlation exists between the form (or design) and a tone; for the archetypal tones sound continuously in the World of Thought (Second Heaven). Occult scientists have pointed out long since that there is a very well-known physical analogy to this heaven world process. If sand is placed on a sheet of glass or brass, and across the edge of it is drawn a violin bow, the sound will cause the sand to form patterns which, in the science of acoustics, are called "the figures of Chladni." The figures vary when the plate is bowed at one point or another.

In the dense, rigid conditions of the physical world these three processes—sound, color and design or form—are separated from one another. In the soul world they occur simultaneously and automatically, in consonance with the laws governing inner realms. Thus it may happen that when an Invisible Helper is awake to a degree in the astral plane while his body sleeps in the physical, he suddenly realizes that music is pouring from objects all about him.

Perhaps he awakens in his soul body to find himself in an art gallery where he sees many beautiful pictures of the Christ here reproduced through the reflective powers of the astral plane. As he gazes upon them there will be a burst of music like that of a great pipe organ. It pours out from the pictures and seems to fill all space. What is this music? It is the higher dimension of the pictures, the equivalent of them in terms of sound—as it is known in the higher heaven where sound dominates. In other words, the Christ pictures are painted in music.

Since we live at all times, not only in the physical world but in the higher soul dimensions which interpenetrate it, every one of us has a deep intuitive knowledge of these facts regarding the soul world. This has always been known to members of Mystery Schools. Plato taught that the love of beauty is but the soul's remembrance of what it once knew before it was encased in flesh.

The Russian composer Scriabin was profoundly interested in the study of color and music. At the time of his transition he was working upon what he hoped would be his masterpiece, a symphony in which the two would be blended. His idea was to place a screen upon the stage above the orchestra. As the symphony was performed, colors would appear simultaneously upon the screen. His passing was a great loss to the New Age art of combining color and music, for he was a gifted pioneer in this most fascinating field of endeavor. The following table is Scriabin's correlation of musical notes with colors as he saw them:

Musical Key	Correlating Color
C	Red
C#	Violet
D	Yellow
D#	Glint of Steel
E	Pearly Blue & Shimmer of Moonlight
F	Dark Red
F#	Bright Blue
G	Rosy Orange
G#	Purple
A	Green
A#	Glint of Steel
B	Soft Blue

The Rainbow Dance

"You have your eyes, you have your ears: look with your eyes on the things of Nature, hear with your ears what goes on in Nature; the spiritual reveals itself through color and through tone, and as you look and listen, you cannot help feeling how it reveals itself in these." —*Rudolf Steiner*

On the radio the question was asked recently: "What is Truth?" A physical scientist replied, "Truth is only that which can be evidenced through sensory perception." How blind and benighted can man be! All Nature is striving to reveal to him something of the wondrous miracles with which he is surrounded, yet he is contented to live in the narrow prison house of his five senses. To such a one we suggest a careful perusal of the words written by that eminent occult scientist, Rudolf Steiner, as he describes to his pupil the inner workings of a rainbow:

"People gaze open-eyed at the rainbow. But if you look at the rainbow with a little imagination, you may see there elemental Beings. These elemental Beings are full of activity and demonstrate it in a very remarkable manner. Here (at yellow) you see some of them streaming forth from the rainbow, continually coming away out of it. They move across and the moment they reach the lower end of the green they are drawn to it again. To one who views it with imagination, the whole rainbow manifests a streaming out of spirit and a disappearing of it again within. It is like a spiritual dance, in very deed a spiritual waltz, wonderful to behold. And you may observe too how these spiritual Beings come forth from the rainbow with terrible fear, and how they go in with invincible courage. When you look at the red-yellow, you see fear streaming out, and when you look at the blue-violet you have the feeling: there is all courage and bravery of heart.

"Now picture to yourselves: There before me is no mere rainbow! Beings are coming out of it and disappearing into it—here anxiety and fear, there courage . . . And now, here the rainbow receives a certain thickness and you will be able to imagine how this gives rise to the element of Water. In this watery element spiritual Beings live, Beings that are actually a kind of copy of the Beings of the Third Hierarchy."

All the manifestations of color which occur in both the inner and outer realms of this earthly planet are under the supervision and direction of the three great Hierarchies, namely, Sagittarius, the Lords of Mind; Capricorn, the Archangels; Aquarius, the Angels.

Evidently the poet Robert Browning had developed some of his extended faculties which enabled him to penetrate into the inner realms when he wrote:

> Only the prism obstruction shows aright
> The secret of the sunbeam:
> Breaks its light into the jewelled bow for blanket white.
> So may a glory from defect arise.

Lumia—A New Art Form

During the last few decades a number of instruments have been invented for the purpose of synchronizing color and tone. Among the most successful of these inventions is that of Mr. Thomas Wilfred, named the *Clavilux*. Many persons reading these lines will recall the pleasurable interest with which they attended the Clavilux concerts. The following account descriptive of Mr. Wilford's work is taken by permission from the August, 1962, issue of *The Journal of Borderland Research*:

A completely new form of art, called Lumia, has been created for the reception room of Clairol's New York offices, 666 Fifth Ave., by Mr. Thomas Wilfred. Moving colors are projected on a ten-foot screen to give the illusion of an abstract painting being created in space, as the tints and shapes swirl through a pre-determined series of patterns. The vivid colors, slowly moving across and through the screen in combination with more delicate hues, create an unusual visual experience which may be watched for seconds, minutes or hours. The procession of color constellations is set to run for one year, 34 weeks, 22 hours and 10 minutes, and then start all over again and exactly repeat the composition.

The "light mobile" is called *Study in Depths, Opus* 152. Mr. Wilfred previously created 151 compositions. These other works are in the Museum of Modern Art, Metropolitan Museum of Art, San Francisco Museum and many in private collections. The Clairol Lumia composition is the largest, will run the longest, and is the first in an office."

A recorded Lumia composition of 1955, gift of Mr. and Mrs. Julius Stulman to the Museum of Modern Art, New York City, is of interest:

Lumia, the art of light, was developed by Thomas Wilfred who experimented for years during the first quarter of a century. In 1921 he completed his "clavilux," an instrument consisting of a number of powerful projectors with an organ-like keyboard controlling the form, color and motion projected on a large white screen. In 1922, in New York, Wilfred performed his first Lumia recital on the clavilux and for 20 years thereafter he gave clavilux recitals throughout the United States, Canada and Europe. In 1930 he founded the Art Institute of Light for the study and further development of this new medium. The Institute maintained laboratories and a recital hall in New York until the war years.

Thomas Wilfred continues his work in Lumia, creating new compositions and recording them for automatic repetition in instruments such as "Aspiration" as shown at the Museum of Modern Art. The artist describes this work as a theme with 397 variations. The form and color cycles are of different duration. Thus every time the form cycle repeats, it does so with a different color treatment—a near coincidence every two hours and 32 minutes. The entire composition has a duration of 42 hours, 14 minutes, 11 seconds.

Of Lumia, the art of light, Mr. Wilfred says:

"Man has built with stone, carved with marble, painted with ground pigments, blown through reeds, plucked strings, sung, danced, written and spoken. Thus our seven fine arts have grown along with our civilization. Their tools and media were both simple and close at hand. One medium, however, defied man's harnessing attempts: Light, the greatest natural force our senses can grasp, the source and maintainer of all life and growth.

"But with the advent of electricity a way opened up, and now a great new epoch begins in esthetics. An eighth major art form has been born to join the accepted seven, the art of light. It has been named Lumia. Here light is the artist's sole medium of expression. He must mold it by optical means, almost as a sculptor models in clay. He must add color and finally motion to his creation.

"Motion, the time dimension, demands that he must be a choreographer in space, a dancer-by-proxy whose body is weightless and may assume any desired shape. This he accomplishes by manipulating sliding form, color and motion keys on the organ-like console of a clavilux instrument. A special notation system is used. The keys actuate optical combinations in a battery of powerful projections, the result showing on a large white screen.

"The Lumia composer may also record his works for automatic repetition in self-contained cabinets resembling television sets. The artist's aim is to transform the screen into a large window looking out on infinite space, an imaginary stage of astronomical dimensions, and to perform on this stage a silent visual music of form, color and motion.

"Further information can be obtained from Thomas Wilfred at West Nyack, New York."

Healing Techniques for the Aquarian Age

Sensitives will be, perhaps, the ones most benefited by New Age color instruments, and the number of sensitives is multiplying rapidly—which means that the whole population will require someday the healing directly brought down from heaven to earth in this way. Children of tender years, and those not yet born, can be influenced by colors affecting the lives of their mothers. The powers latent in both color and tone possess almost infinite possibilities for benefiting humanity. When this fact has been generally accepted, work with color and tone will be a most important factor in the daily treatment programs of hospitals and schools. When parents, doctors and teachers are wise enough to substitute their constructive values for the dull fabrics and blatant current trends in music, a new era in culture, healing and education will be opened up to all, especially children. Those of average intelligence will become precocious and the problems of delinquency will rapidly decline. A wiser and more responsible generation will then bless the earth.

May the following list of compositions assist students in selecting music for their periods of meditation:

Meditation from Thais, Massenet; *Ave Maria*, Bach-Gounod; Grail Music of Wagner; Masses and Gospels set to music by various composers; favorite hymns in a tender mood.

Blue, blue-violet, lavender and purple should be used with the above devotional background music. Meditation for unfolding inner power calls for initiatory music and color tones of blue, indigo, violet, purple and amethyst. Suggested compositions:

The Ring Cycle — Wagner; *Parsifal, Lohengrin* —Wagner; *Orpheus and Eurydice, Alceste*—Gluck; *The Magic Flute*—Mozart; *Thais*—Massenet; *Aida*—Verdi; The Nine Symphonies of Beethoven; *Swan Lake, Sleeping Beauty*—Tschaikowsky.

Also, there are fine recordings of readings from the great classics of literature and religion, in both prose and poetry, which lend themselves to meditation when accompanied by appropriate colors and musical compositions.

WAGNER—A TONAL AND COLOR SENSITIVE

Richard Wagner was especially aware of the sensitizing and refining influence of color on mind and body. Next to his body he wore only silk, and this in carefully chosen colors to harmonize with the type of composition upon which he was currently engaged. This was not just an eccentricity. It was a case of a nervous system which had become responsive to color's subtle radiation beyond the ordinary range of human sensitivity. In his most inspired moments Wagner felt the need of the emanations that came from delicate pastel colors, such as orchid, blues, crystalline and pale mauves and the rich golden tones which, to the soul sense, characterize the songs of Angels and seem almost to power their flight through the celestial spaces. His own color note was purple.

PART IV

**COLOR AND MUSIC
OF THE FOUR SACRED SEASONS**

CHAPTER VII

The Spring Equinox

George Frederic Handel's *Messiah*
Richard Wagner's *Parsifal*

Spiritual High Points of the Year

he four Sacred Seasons mark definite power releases upon the earth. During the four-day interval introducing each of these Seasons the currents of desire are largely stilled so the spiritual forces can predominate. Hence, these are the most propitious periods of the year for an aspirant to make dedications to a spiritual life, and for a disciple to extend his dedication to a wider field of service upon both the inner and outer planes.

Richard Wagner was an inspired musical Initiate who knew how to attune himself to the mighty powers directed earthward during these Sacred Seasons. The music he correlated with each transitional point is attuned to its vibratory rhythms and, therefore, it greatly aids a disciple in unfolding his latent powers; also in interpreting and deepening his soul-realization.

The two Equinoxes and the two Solstices are the high points of the year. All nature comes into attunement with spiritual energies released at these times. When sufficiently sensitized, man too will avail himself of them to further his spiritual development. Artists, writers, poets, musicians and other creative workers often merge themselves with the inspiration to be found therein, with the result that the masterpieces they give to the world are endowed with a downpouring of the same energies.

For example, in *Midsummer Night's Dream* Shakespeare describes the beauty, joy and elation prevailing at the Summer Solstice. In *Paradise Lost Milton* depicts the darkness which descends upon earth with the Autumnal Equinox. Tennyson's *Idylls of the King* are reminiscent of the glory attendant upon the coming of the archangelic King at the time of the Winter Solstice. And Wagner's magnificent soul-drama *Parsifal* is radiant with the resurrection light of the Spring Equinox.

"Parsifal" and the Mystery of the Holy Grail

Correlated to the Spring Equinox, *Parsifal* is a soul-drama built around the occult significance of Good Friday. In the esoteric meaning of Good Friday is concealed the real import of the Easter rites. The Holy Grail music of both *Parsifal* and *Lohengrin* is a transcription of celestial harmonies, and has its place with the most sacred music ever conveyed to this earthly realm.

The Mystery of the Holy Grail is the secret heart of this seasonal point, and it has always been the innermost core of Temple teachings. For the first time in the history of mankind, however, *Parsifal* laid bare to an unprecented degree the long hidden meaning of the Grail so that whomsoever will may come and partake of its wondrous knowledge. The Sacred Spear and the Holy Grail Cup are keys to both the unsurpassed music-drama and the Spring Equinox.

In spring time nature is resplendent with new life. Its beauty is bodied forth in every slender stem rising from the tomb of earth to be crowned by a shining flowery cup, thus proclaiming through color and fragrance the exultant resurrection message to all who will give heed. This same sacred symbol appears within the body of man, for through the spinal column ascends the Spirit Fire to be crowned with the glory of an illumined head center—since in regenerate and redeemed man that center is transformed into a "flower" of rarest splendor.

The most profound Mysteries ever given to humanity are the Mysteries of the Grail Cup. They prefigure the Mysteries of all ages and all nations. Their impress was set upon ancient Lemuria and

Atlantis. They were used in the Mysteries of Babylon and Egypt and Greece. It was the Mysteries of the Grail that the Master taught to His most advanced Disciples in the evening of His Resurrection. And throughout the world today the Grail's hallowed rites are performed upon innumerable altars dedicated to the Christ. But the deepest Mysteries concealed within the Blessed Cup will not be revealed in their entirety until the world has entered more fully into the New Age.

The character of Parsifal typifies an aspirant who sets out upon the quest of high attainment. He is called the "Mystic Fool" because all who set their feet to the Path are termed fools by the worldly wise. Before Parsifal comes into possession of the Sacred Spear he, like Amfortas, the white knight who was tested and failed, is also tempted and tried by the glamor and illusions of the sense plane. Few are the aspirants who pass this first subtle trial. For those who fail the Grail Cup and the Sacred Spear remain mere legendary myths.

Parsifal further symbolizes the rare soul who succeeds in reaching Mastership. When he finally gains possession of the Sacred Spear, he declares that he will use it "never to hurt but only to heal." In this statement he gives a most important key to the attainment of self-mastery. Having acquired the *spear* within his own body-temple, the Knight is found worthy to become the leader of all the other Grail Knights (aspirants on the Path) and to be their guide and teacher along the way leading to Mastership. With this Spear—symbol of the spinal Spirit Fire when, through regeneration, it is lifted from the sacral plexus to the head center—Parsifal heals Amfortas who is suffering from a wound "in his side" inflicted by the same Spear. Amfortas represents humanity, for man also suffers from a wound "in his side," that area of the body-temple wherein is located the seed atom of desire. Misdirected desire currents brought about the "fall" of mankind and still subject the race to every ill to which flesh is heir, and even to death. Healing from this "fallen" state can come only at the touch of the Sacred Spear; in other words, by means of spiritual powers resulting from a regenerated life. Having accomplished such regeneration, Parsifal is able to focus the energy for healing Amfortas.

The radiance and power of the Cosmic Grail reach earth in special measure at the Spring Equinox, manifesting its sheer beauty and brilliance in the equinoctial Full Moon as it rises above the eastern horizon. Its mystic radiations are preparatory to the kindling of the resurrectional fires that come into full glory on Easter Morn. Appropriate spiritual observances of the Spring Equinox will greatly assist the aspirant to enter into attunement with the heightened and uplifting activities of this blessed Cosmic Grail.

During the month of March—which comes under the mystical sign of the Zodiac, Pisces—the out-pouring of the Cosmic Grail upon our Northern Hemisphere manifests as a rising tide of life in all the kingdoms of nature. Bursting buds, miniature grail cups, have a correspondence in man. Both give promise of a flowering to follow as the result of their appropriation of the impulse thus released.

Of all the Knights who came to Mt. Salvat, Parsifal alone is qualified to use the Sacred Spear to heal. His attainment is such that he is adjudged worthy to stand in the presence of Raphael—the Archangel of healing who reigns over the first quarter of the year—and to receive from him mystic Grail powers.

The Eucharist is the very heart of the Spring Equinox mystery. Its sacred feast is the climatic note of *Parsifal*, Wagner's great music-drama. Then it is that the Lord Christ is released from bondage within the earth; and as He ascends, the entire planet is flooded with His transforming spirit. At the same time a tremendous spiritual force pours down from the Sun, vitalizing all growing things by its radiance. In very truth, the sacrificial bread is the Lord's body, and the wine is His blood which He sheds for all mankind.

Such is the vision that exalts the Grail Knights when Parsifal unveils the Holy Cup, the very Cup that has caused Amfortas intense anguish from the moment his spiritual sight waned as a result of his yielding to sensual desire. But he is now healed by the touch of the Sacred Spear, in the hand of Parsifal. A like healing awaits all men in the hour of their great over-coming, for true regeneration banishes the pain, sorrow, disease and fear of death that now plagues the human race. Then are fulfilled the prophetic words of St. John, "The former things are passed away."

At the ceremonial of the Holy Feast, surrounded by Knights kneeling about him in reverential devotion, Parsifal stands before the Holy of Holies, his being illumined by a transcendent light emanating from the Grail Cup. Upon the triumphant healing of Amfortas and of the chorusing of jubilant Angels, Wagner's magnificent soul drama of the Resurrection Mysteries reaches its closing climax.

Song of the Resurrection

To the average person the phrase "Music of the Spheres" is a mere poetic fantasy. To an esoteric student, however, it has a profound and holy significance. Physical scientists state that motion is accompanied by sound. Esoteric scientists recognize that there is music in the waving of grass, a song as leaves are wafted by a breeze, and a symphony beyond compare in the unfolding of flower petals.

The resurrection fiat of the Cosmic Christ resounds throughout all nature at the time of the Spring Equinox: "And I, if I be lifted up from the earth, will draw all men unto me." Nature responds to this call. From out the dark tomb of winter, resurrected life force streams forth in a flood of glory. So rhythmic is the ascending life current that its harmonies are the most exultant of the entire year. The currents rise in perfect "chromatics of ecstasy" until, at the Easter sunrise, they reach a climactic point in a tremendous outpouring of sound, color and fragrance that unites with the triumphal chorusing of Hosts of Angels. Both heaven and earth reverberate with this resurrection anthem.

Unfortunately, mankind cannot hear this celestial symphony. But individuals sense in varying degrees its effect, and this is why the most impressive musical events of the year are expressive of the Easter Season. In this we note how intimately man's outer life is governed by inner-plane occurrences. Down through the ages, however, there have been those who have caught fragments of the heavenly ensemble and then transcribed them for human hearing.

Such an one was Handel. In the ecstatic measures of his *Hallelujah Chorus* from *The Messiah* he caught something of the exaltation of resurrection music.

Rhythms of inner-plane resurrection music never change. It was to these same rhythms that priests of Ancient Egypt and their neophytes, gathered on the banks of the Nile, intoned a hymn to the Sun God Ra as they celebrated the Feast of the Spring Equinox; and teachers of future ages will assemble their disciples for rhythmic celebrations of the Eastertide. Times, manners and customs change but the harmonies of nature are immutable and eternal. The cosmic Sunrise is resonant with the songs of Angels proclaiming triumphantly "He is risen," to which all nature responds in an upsurge of newly awakened life. From the glory of this floodtide of resurrection music man's soul receives fresh intimations of the risen life, and thereby brings his being into closer harmony with nature and nature's God.

When its guiding Angel sounds the keynote of spring, the life force in bulbs and roots—which has been dormant during the winter months—awakens and begins an upward ascent. In its spiralling motion this rising force is attuned to music in a major key, strong, joyous and infused with rapture. Etherically, this ascending force may be seen as a filmy, silvery-green essence, the exquisite colortone with which nature heralds the coming of spring.

Raphael, archangelic custodian of vernal activities, is often depicted holding in his outstretched hands the Cosmic Grail containing the alchemical impulses to become manifest in their full beauty and glory. As man comes into at-one-ment with this divine upsurge transmitting the energies which Raphael, also Archangel of Healing, brings to earth at this time of renewal. In this healing radiation resides the secret of a universal panacea that humanity is destined to possess for healing the ills of the world.

The secret of healing is concealed in the process of transmutation which, in turn, is to be found in the mystery of Golgotha—for the Christ is the Great Physician embodying the only true healing principle. This principle is available for use by all individuals to the degree that they establish themselves in harmonious relationship with the redemptive Healer, the Lord Christ.

The Spiritual Impact of Handel's "Messiah"

As a tuning fork that is pitched to a certain vibration will start to sing when another of the same key is struck, so also will it be with us; when we have been attuned to the vibrations of the Christ, we shall be able to express the love that He came to teach mankind. Until we live up to that love and perceive the Christ within, we cannot see the Christ without.

—Max Heindel

One of the greatest achievements in the history of music is Handel's *Messiah*. It was the outcome of pure inspiration. The whole oratorio was set down under a most intense and concentrated application extending over a period of only twenty-four days. During this time the composer scarcely ate or slept. He was all but out of this world. His mind was in a trance. He did not leave his home. His servant brought him food and, as often as not, returned to his room to find it untouched and his master staring into space. When Handel had completed Part II, it is recorded, his servant found him at his table, tears streaming from his eyes. "I think I did see all of heaven before me, and the great God Himself," Handel exclaimed.

Handel divided *The Messiah* into three sections. Part I contains a prophecy of the Nativity in a narrative about the event. Part II recounts the Passion and the Resurrection, reaching a magnificent culmination in the *Hallelujah Chorus*. Part III sounds forth the Christ power within man himself, the power whereby he will attain his own personal resurrection.

By reason of the great spiritual illumination which inspired this music, Handel never considered it his own and would not, therefore, accept any remuneration for it. Whatever returns came to him he donated to hospitals, orphanages and prisons; to the Foundling Hospital of London he bequeathed all royalties accruing from the oratorio.

The *Shepherd's Chorus* in this composition is said to be attuned to the rhythms sung by Initiate-shepherds at the Christ Child's birth on that first Holy Night. It is purported that the earlier song is still in existence, having been preserved in Rome, and that it was made accessible to Handel on one of his many visits to that city.

Tenderness, purity, grandeur and an almost prophetic up-liftment characterize *The Messiah*. Moral force and spiritual power flow from its tonal patterns, and this is what Handel hoped for his composition. Once, when a friend complimented him on the work, Handel replied, "I should be sorry if I only entertained them; I wish to make them better." In this Handel did not hope in vain.

Throughout the world a realization of the deep and lasting worth of Handel's opus has increased until now, especially at the Christmas and Easter Seasons, *The Messiah* is heard wherever voices are raised in praise and adoration of the Blessed Lord. The beneficial effect of music on man has been demonstrated beyond doubt by this superb composition. Through its influence persons have been inspired to reform and entire communities have been up-lifted. Two concrete instances are recorded which substantiate the latter claim.

Some years ago it was reported that in Lindsborg, Kansas, *The Messiah* had been given every Eastertide for something like three-quarters of a century. Rehearsals extended all through the year with participants drawn from the homes of the community at large. To this specific activity is linked the fact that there was a period when the local jail had been without an occupant for so long the people had come to regard it as useless.

The Lindsborg experience has a musical parallel in another Kansas community, which was reported in *Reader's Digest* under the caption *Mad About Music*. This occurred in the town of Winfield, where music has entered into the very fabric of the citizen's lives since the early eighties. According to the article, "delinquency is a curiosity and night clubs have been unable to get a start among high school youth."

Comparable to the presentation of *The Messiah* in Lindsborg every Easter is its London performance every Good Friday in Albert Hall, one of England's annual musical highlights.

The Messiah is a sacred opera. It might well be designated a miracle in music, one in which Angels participated that they might share with man their secrets relative to tone and color. These angelic secrets have encircled the earth with streams of golden tonal light that bring healing to the sick and hope to the despairing; and that awaken in all who hear their sublime strains a deeper realization of innate divinity. In the *Hallelujah Chorus* a thousand throats proclaim the triumph of their Lord, while *Forever Worthy Is the Lamb* voices the gratitude of the redeemed. In the grand finale the music of the *Amen Chorus* mounts to levels of majestic grandeur. One word only can express the emotional response in the hearts of Christian disciples and that word is a grand and glorious AMEN!

It is most fitting that Handel's color note is a luminous white high-lighted with silver.

CHAPTER VIII

The Summer Solstice

Mendelssohn's *Midsummer Night's Dream*
Wagner's *Die Meistersinger*

Zodiacal Correlations

uring the time that the disciple is working for Purification in the interval of the Autumn Equinox, the accompanying music which permeates all nature is that of Libra.

During the Winter Solstice as one works with the development of the love center in the heart the accompanying nature music is that of the Hierarchy of Capricorn.

During the Spring Equinox the energies generated in meditation enter the larynx and strengthen this creative center as a matrix of increasing spiritual power. The music is that of the Hierarchy of Aries.

During the Summer Solstice when the work is centered in illuminating the head centers the music is that of the Hierarchy of Cancer.

Seasonal Colors

The colors of the Summer Solstice on the inner plane is a soft azure blue while the outer physical world is bathed in streamers of pulsing gold, the Christ's own Ray. It is in this soft golden Ray that He enfolds the entire earth in His blessing during the whole time of the Feast of the Ascension.

Periods of meditative prayer during these four Sacred Seasons will be greatly augmented and strengthened by the accompaniment of the appropriate seasonal music.

As the Spring color note is silver, so that of Summer is gold. The silver of Spring is united with and transformed into vast shimmering rays of molten gold. It is this golden Ray which Angels and Archangels work with to infuse earth's inner realms during the Autumn Equinox, and which centers in the heart of the earth at Christmas time.

One sufficiently illumined at this time can enter into divine at-one-ment with the cosmos. On Midsummer's Day he becomes a part of the great cosmic Mystery.

From Spring to Summer, the spiritual forces become more luminously beautiful and at the same time more powerfully spiritual. Man, if awakened spiritually, comes increasingly to be a part of this great rhapsody of Nature.

Mendelssohn's Music from "Midsummer Night's Dream"

Felix Mendelssohn was perhaps the only one of the celebrated composers who did not know the whiplash of poverty. He was born into a family of affluence and was reared amid serene and congenial surroundings. It was in the expansive grounds of his family estate that he found inspiration for composing much of his music. This was a particularly ideal environment for composing the very beautiful music for *Midsummer Night's Dream.* It was in his own spacious garden that this music was first rendered with Mendelssohn himself conducting.

This composer's color note is a clear beautiful pink. This accords not only with the color tone of his music but also that of his personal life since he was truly privileged to view life through rose-colored glasses.

Most people regard Shakespeare's *Midsummer Night's Dream* as pure fanciful entertainment. It is that, but much more. Beneath the surface of this fairy-land fantasy, Shakespeare has interwoven one of the most profoundly spiritual messages to be found in any of his works.

Many famous composers and musicians who have reached a high place in their profession have been occult scientists and deeply interested in studying the inner side of life and nature. We do not know if Mendelssohn is in this category; but if not his intuitive genius enabled him to weave into his music all the delightful merriment and frivolity of the little fairy folk together with the high and serious dedication to the things of spirit—as he did, for instance, in the famous Wedding March. The supreme ideal of every marriage should be the union of the lower nature with the higher which is known esoterically as the Mystic Marriage, and this it is that sounds the high keynote of *Midsummer Night's Dream.*

As we have many times observed, there is a great inflow of spiritual energies at the time of the four Sacred Seasons, namely, the Summer and Winter Solstices and the Spring and Autumn Equinoxes. The Summer Solstice is the highest spiritual season of the entire year. In fact, the energies it releases are so high and its ideals so transcendent that they are generally unrecognized by the great majority. To the serious student of spiritual science it is a time of rare opportunity for soul quickening. This inner stimulation can be substantially accentuated by meditation to the accompaniment of Mendelssohn's *Midsummer Night's* Music.

Children would profit from an acquaintance with Shakespeare's exposition of fairyland joys and frolics as these are accentuated by Mendelssohn's accompanying music. In this perfect blend of story and music conditions are created favorable to the development of the higher and finer qualities of character with which to meet the problems of maturer years.

Song of the Ascension

For an intuitive aspirant as well as an illumined disciple the four Sacred Seasons sound a clarion call to "come up higher." At these four seasons heaven and earth are in closest attunement. It is the time when clairvoyants and Initiates are born, for the wonders of heaven then lie open to men of earth that they may know what is biblically described as "the things which God hath prepared for them that love him."

Many sacred scriptures make reference to holy events that

occurred at these yearly points of significance. Wise men of all ages have taught their disciples to receive illumination according to their capacity at these special times. The highest teaching ever given to humanity is the Sermon on the Mount, delivered at the Summer Solstice. Man must learn to apply the transcendent truths of this sermon in his daily life if he would be numbered among pioneers worthy to receive the Christ at His second coming.

The Ascension is likewise correlated with the Summer Solstice, when all nature, every tree, shrub and plant, bursts forth in an ecstasy of golden glory—a radiant aura as a signal to the stars. Angels chant in gladsome hosannas and fairies frolic in a perfect abandon of delight. Heaven itself sets an impress of ineffable beauty upon the whole earth. At the Ascension the Christ rises to His own world of Life Spirit, the World of Christed Consciousness. This is the realm of eternal oneness and harmony. The exaltation of consciousness belonging to this realm enables the Christ to declare, "I and my Father are one."

The Feast of Pentecost also correlates with the Summer Solstice. Midsummer marks the perfect fruiting of nature's work of the year as the Feast of the Pentecost marks the ultimate attainmnet of man's spiritual evolvement during the earth period. The Lord Christ came as the supreme Way-shower, and those who walked closely in His steps were the Immortal Twelve. During the Feast of Pentecost they followed Him to His own realm of Christed Consciousness—a state beyond all divisions, dissensions, inharmony. Here an aspirant experiences the "allness of one and the oneness of all." It is this perfect oneness that enabled the Disciples to understand and speak all languages. The secrets of heaven and earth were revealed to them and they spoke truths of which they had had no previous concept. In this exaltation of consciousness they were able to understand and to demonstrate for themselves the statement of the Master when He said, "I am in the Father, and the Father in me."

Spiritually sensitive aspirants realize that certain specific forces are released at the time of the four Sacred Seasons. These powers are focused directly upon certain vital centers within man's body-temple. Awakening these centers constitutes the work of discipleship and their full maturity attests the attainment of Initiateship.

The radiation that plays upon an individual at the Autumn Equinox is that of purification. It acts directly upon the sacral center located at the base of the spine. It is thus that the work of regeneration begins.

The predominating Ray that beams its influence upon earth at the Winter Solstice is that which transmits the power of love. The Christmas Festival is the Love Feast of the year. It has its center in the heart of man.

The spiritual energies that envelop the earth at the Spring Festival are resonant with power and focus upon the creative center in man's body, the larynx. By this organ the divine creative word will be generated in the new race body.

The primary Ray that envelops earth at the Summer Solstice is a radiant stream of light, for this is the supreme Light Festival of the year. This force centers at the top of man's head. When this center is awakened it becomes the heavenly lamp, the light of which never lay on land or sea. It was the lighting of the spiritual lamp that caused a halo of golden radiance to surround the head of each disciple on that sacred occasion known as the Feast of Pentecost.

Wagner's "Die Meistersinger"
And what is so rare as a day in June?
Then if ever, come perfect days.

—James Russell Lowell

So sings the poet. And his words are so applicable to the beauty of the Summer Solstice, when all nature is attired in robes of shimmering light and color and the whole landscape is literally drenched in loveliness. It is at this season of the year that the portals of initiatory Temples swing wide so that all who are worthy may enter in and partake of the waters of eternal life.

The Autumn Equinox, we have learned, is the time when an aspirant passes through disciplines of purification and transmutation, as narrated in *Tannhauser*. *Lohengrin* is descriptive of the Winter Solstice, when a victorious disciple comes to stand in the presence of a great Master. It is only after one has passed through this sublime experience that he can understand the true significance of the words: "He was not that Light, but was sent to bear witness to that Light. That was the true Light, which lighteth every man that cometh into the world." John 1:8,9.

The real import of the Sacred Cup is given at the Spring Equinox in its relation both to the holy temple of man's body and to the workings of nature all about him. Then, with the Summer Solstice, comes the most glorious of all Temple rites, the Rite of the Mystic Marriage. The music drama, *Die Meistersinger*, is attuned to this final exalted degree in all its ceremonial beauty.

Die Meistersinger is a song of the Summer Solstice. Events depicted therein occur within the four-day interval of that seasonal turning point. In it are indicated the more subtle tests and temptations which beset the path of a more advanced disciple. These tests are not of the objective plane so much as of his own consciousness and they are related to the development of discrimination, compassion, obedience and understanding. The gloriously beautiful and triumphant *Prize Song* sounds the exultation of a successful seeker. Truly it is the initiatory song of the Summer Solstice.

As used by Wagner in his opera, the term "meistersinger" denotes one who has attained to mastership by Initiation through music. In *Tristan and Isolde* the musical seer gives definite instruction for preparation leading up to this Rite of the Mystic Marriage depicted in *Die Meistersinger*.

In the overture to the latter the three most important themes are closely related to the Summer Solstice. They are the *Mastersinger's Chorus*, the *Song of Love* and the *Song of Spring*. Uriel, that glorified celestial Being who stands guardian at the Summer Solstice, is known as the Angel of Love, and the *Song of Love* is his keynote. This Angelic One is always accompanied by the Angel of Beauty, the Angel of Vision and the Angel of Truth.

The *Song of Spring* is the musical keynote of the Spring Equinox. Raphael then assumes guardianship over the year's quarter that follows. At the time of the Summer Solstice this Archangel relinquishes His guardianship over Nature to Uriel, the midsummer Angel. In the opera, the *Song of Spring*, which sounds Raphael's keynote, can be heard echoing and re-echoing until it finally seems to be lost amidst the infinitude of cosmic space, while the *Song of Love* emanating from Uriel, the midsummer Angel, permeates the music. It is through the musical pulsations sent forth by the four mighty Beings governing the four Sacred Seasons that nature is sustained in its flourishing creative processes.

The opening scene of *Die Meistersinger* occurs within the majestic Cathedral of St. Catherine. The chorus is chanting the beautiful measures of a St. John chorale. In early Christian times the festivities of the Summer Solstice were dedicated to St. John the Baptist, to whom the Christ paid tribute in the words: "Among them that are born of women there hath not arisen one greater than John the Baptist." This St. John music forms an exquisite background to the many themes of the opera from its first to its closing scenes.

Within the cathedral is the young Knight, Walter, representative of an aspirant to the Rite of the Mystic Marriage. He is attracted to the lovely maiden, Eva, who typifies his higher nature, for it is only in man's union with his spiritual counterpart that this holy rite can be consummated. Walter, the disciple, must create a prize song before he can win the hand of Eva and be admitted to the Mastersinger's Guild. Hans Sachs, leader of the Mastersingers, becomes his spiritual teacher as he prepares for this great honor. Beckmesser, villain of the drama, typifies man's lower nature. His musical theme is discordant and his entrances produce an air of inharmony and confusion. This is ever true of man's lower nature until it is lifted up and transmuted by the power of his spirit.

In anticipation of the contest about to take place under the supervision of Hans Sachs, Walter and Eva are arrayed in nuptial attire (luminous aura of light). Their dedication by the Master Teacher takes place to some of the most exquisite music ever heard in our earthly sphere. It is truly celestial music that was once heard only in Temples of Initiation.

The music-drama reaches its culmination during this act when, in the presence of a joyous and festive assemblage, Walter sings his

Prize Song. The entire scene is made superb by the *Mastersingers' Chorus* and the enchanting *Song of Love*, together with the Saint John Music. Walter's song is an out-pouring of exaltation engendered by his initiatory experience.

In the work depicted in *Tannhauser*, dealing with the Autumn Equinox, the ideal given to the aspirant is expressed through the rod that budded—a vision of the uplifted and transmuted creative spinal fire from the lower area of the aspirant's body to his head, touching each of the seven spiritual centers as it ascends. Through the work of the Summer Solstice and the celebration of the Mystic Marriage, the aspirant (Walter in the opera) enters celestial realms and there sees a glorious tree illumined by brilliant stars. His body has now become wholly spiritualized and these centers revolve as they radiate light and color. (Herein lies the deeper meaning of the Christmas tree, which had its origin in celebration of the Winter Solstice when it was a true Christ Mass.) In the light of this glorious tree, Walter and Eva are united for all time. In other words, the drama portrays the sublime culmination of the Midsummer Solstice in the Mystic Marriage.

Each step on the Path of Attainment has its own particular Initiation. That bestowed at the time of the Summer Solstice is *continuity of consciousness.* Never again will the aspirant who has entered into the Mystic Marriage experience a period of unconsciousness between sleeping and waking, between death and rebirth. Various events in the life of the Christ are keys to these initiatory experiences. The one which correlates with the Summer Solstice is the Ascension, when the Master passed in unbroken consciousness from this earth plane into the higher cosmic realms.

At the conclusion of his *Prize Song*, symbolizing the highest phase of man's spiritual attainment, Walter is crowned by Eva (his higher nature) with a radiant halo of light indicative of his having become a true Master Singer.

CHAPTER IX

The Autumn Equinox

Bach's *Passion of St. Matthew*
Wagner's *Tannhauser*

Music is a moral law. It gives a soul to the universe, wings to the mind, flight to the imagination, a charm to sadness, gaiety and life to everything. It is the essence of order, and leads to all that is good and just and beautiful.

—Plato

Down-pouring of the Father Ray

 n the autumn season all the earth is resonant with music and vibrant with color. Each of the four Sacred Seasons sounds its own keynote and radiates its own special color. The outer, planetary color of the Autumn Equinox is a soft, exquisite blue like the mist that veils mountain tops at early dawn. Blue transmits power. It is the color of the Father Ray. It creates forms and then when they have served their purpose in the economy of nature they are by this same power resolved into their primordial elements.

The inner color of the autumn season is a soft, golden tone, the Christ Ray which heralds His annual descent into the heart of the earth.

When the Angel of Autumn sounds its spiritual keynote the life-force begins its descent toward the bulbs and roots. Its spiralling descent is attuned to minors—soft, tender, filled with sadness, as the leaves drift gently downward like crimson and golden tears shed for summer's waning beauty. In the words of William Cullen Bryant, it is then "The melancholy days are come, the saddest of the year."

Earth passes through a process of purification and transmutation each year as also do the disciples on the Path. The purification process culminates after the Spring Equinox and the transmutation process after the Summer Solstice. The accumulated evils of earth create a huge psychic entity that takes the form of a cosmic dragon which has the same relation to earth's humanity as does the Dweller on the Threshold to the individual. These are self-generated entities that must be overcome by humanity as a whole in the one case and by the individual in the other as each and all advance on the way that leads to ultimate liberation and Illumination.

Michael's Cleansing Activities

In the autumn season when the Archangel Michael presides over the last quarter of the year His service is to assist mankind in overcoming the Dragon it has created and that stands in the way of its spiritual attainment. The biblical account of Michael's battle with the Dragon was not only a single event in the remote past. It is a battle He continues to wage, and which is resumed with concentrated powers during the autumnal season. Michael's role is redemptive. He stands next in angelic rank to the Lord Christ. His countenance is likened to the brilliance of the Sun.

Michael's radiations are cleansing. They let added light into the earth's atmosphere. And so it is that in the life of the aspirant this is the season to deepen dedication, to turn to the light within that it may increase, though the light without is decreasing, and by overcoming the dragon of his own lower nature, open the way to enter more fully into the golden light on the Path that leads to the heart of the earth at the time of the Winter Solstice.

The Song of Sacrifice

The four great planetary cycles have their parallel in the four principal steps in human birth. In the materialistic thinking current today man has forgotten the significance of the successive stages of development.

The first step of the Birth Ritual is that of the Annunciation and corresponds to the golden ecstasy of the season of the Summer Solstice. At autumn time when the sun passes into Virgo, the earth receives a special measure of the golden inflow of the Christ Spirit. The hosts of Virgo are the foci for this celestial golden outpouring. As this Christed light floods the etheric sheaths of the planet, all the plant kingdom becomes luminous with its light. To a spiritually sensitive person, September is the most fitting time in which to hold high communion with Nature. In the reverent and awe-inspiring sacred hush of this season the earth experiences the wonder of the planetary Immaculate Conception.

At the Autumn Equinox the golden Christ Ray blends with the blue, and the atmosphere is suffused with a rare light of shimmering blue-gold. Now it is that the celestial Hosts of Libra join in the heavenly hallelujahs, for as the Christ force touches the outermost edge of the earth's physical envelope, the sacred moment of the quickening occurs. All the planet is touched with a new life impulse, and its vibratory rhythms are lifted.

The time from the Autumn Equinox to the Winter Solstice are days for the aspirant to walk consciously in the Christ light that is then penetrating deeper into the earth until it is focused at the very heart of the earth at the time of the Winter Solstice (December 21) and reaching its climax on December 24 when jubilant hosts chant the midnight birth of a new Sun. Thus when observed spiritually the earth planet is immersed in a rainbow of color and a symphony of sound.

Two of the sacred seasons, the Spring Equinox and the Summer Solstice, ray forth colors which are brilliant and vivid, and which are attuned to the majestic tone of a major symphony. The other two sacred seasons, namely the Autumn Equinox and the Winter Solstice, ray forth colors that are soft and luminous, and which are attuned to the tender tones of a minor symphony. Thus we come to note something of our planetary rhythms of light and shadow by major and minor tones in color and sound.

All mankind is affected by these alternating seasons in ways of which they are for the most part as yet quite unconscious. But everyone does experience in his outer life something of these effects. Thus, for example, in Spring and Summer man naturally seeks the open spaces and pursues interests pertaining to the outer objective life. In the Autumn and Winter seasons the interests turn more inward. Life becomes more subjective. Thus for example, our educational system follows this pattern: relaxation in Spring and Summer; study in Autumn and Winter.

The Autumn season is the time for deepening soul dedication, for renewal of soul aspiration. It is a time to tune in with the inner processes of nature and to conform the activities of the inner life to the spiritual character of the season. In this way the aspirant will come into a personal realization of the harmony that exists between the life and character of the Lord Christ and all other world teachers and that of Nature which is God in manifestation. Thus does he come to take on some of these same qualities and to join the ranks of that ever growing number of men and women whose uppermost purpose is to assist the Christ in his redemptive work for humanity and to advance His reign on earth.

Bach's *Passion of St. Matthew*

As previously stated, certain music will be found to be in perfect attunement with one of the four Sacred Seasons. The works of Johann Sebastian Bach are in perfect attunement with the Autumn Equinox; this is the season of dedication and reconsecration of the disciple in preparation for the new spiritual year which lies just ahead. The music of Bach's *Passions of St. Matthew* and *St. John* are particularly harmonious in this dedicatory work.

The events of the Master's Passion have their recapitulation in the lives of the disciples. If the time spent in prayerful meditation upon these events is accompanied by Bach's Passion music, new ideals of attainment will be born within and a new and higher impetus to both spiritual aspiration and inspiration will become a component part of a disciple's life during the interval of this Sacred Season.

The spiritual power incorporated in Passion music is realized when listening to the sublime *Passions* of Bach; one should relax completely and, letting go of all mundane concerns, lift consciousness into harmony with spiritual realms. One will then become conscious of an emotional replenishment, a mental exhilaration and a great spiritual illumination.

Of all arts, esotericists acknowledge noble music to be the highest expression of spirit. Issuing direct from the godhead, every human soul on the path from "clod to God" is a song sung by the Master Musician. We are made of the very substance of divine harmony. Those who have ears to hear may listen to this harmony; and some may transcribe in immortal music the likeness of God in man, *Immanuel*, man's "fall" into materiality, and the path of redemption therefrom—in short, Initiation.

Those composers whose works show forth the undying beauty of spirit—for in that their immortality consists—acquired their great mastery through lifetimes of sorrow and toil. However faulty their personalities may have been, they have, in some degree at least, entered the sanctuary of the Most High, the fount of eternal life, the source of all genius. Hence, whether or not he is wholly aware of the fact, each composer sounds a peculiar, a unique keynote he has heard with the ear of his spirit; and, as all esotericists know, that keynote has a direct bearing upon the composer's own, and upon mankind's, spiritual development. The combined works of such musicians form a magnificent ensemble outlining the Path of Initiation. It is in accordance with his own particular requirements for spiritual progress that an aspirant is drawn to a certain favorite composer.

Bach may well be termed the high priest of abstract music. In other words, he was a channel through which rhythms from the highest heaven (the third heaven of Paul) flow into human souls. To one seeking to obey Paul's injunction concerning the Christing of the mind, the music of Bach is all-important.

Bach's color tone is a clear vibrant blue, which is also the color of the higher or Abstract Mind, and is most nearly depicted on this physical plane in the blue of a gas flame. And blue, as previously stated, is autumn's external color.

An Initiate understands the power released by intoning the name of Christ Jesus. An Initiate-musician combines the power of the sacred Word with the power of rhythm. This combined power is necessary to a true musical depicting of the Passion. Bach, by reason of his magnificent contributions along this line, has been called the supreme poet of tone-speech.

All students of the Ancient Wisdom know that the Gospels contain formulas of Initiation. Speaking of these, Paul refers to them as "milk for babes" and "meat for the strong." These formulas have always been know to the Initiated. Hence, St. Augustine's statement: "that which is called the Christian religion existed among the ancients from the beginning of the human race. With the coming of Christ Jesus true religion began to be called Christianity." Ignatius and Polycarp, disciples of the Beloved John, mention the "inner Mysteries of Jesus" which were known and observed during the first and second centuries of our era. Origen also writes: "The Scriptures have one meaning which is apparent to all men and another which escapes the notice of most men. The spiritual meaning of the Scriptures is not known to all; to His own disciples did the Master open up all things." In the apocryphal Gospel of Matthew, the Master is quoted as saying: "My secret is for me and for the children of my house."

It is the inner significance of the Gospel which is portrayed in Bach's Passion. Each event in the life of the Master is attuned to its own specific keynote. Placing ourselves in harmony with that keynote will enable us to view in the etheric records the actual happening as it is inscribed therein.

An Initiate-musician not only hears celestial music but he also sees pictures which accompany it. It is for this reason that highly sensitized musicians and artists are in such close accord. A spiritual artist creates corresponding rhythmic color-patterns upon his canvas. Perhaps the greatest modern painter of initiatory truths was Nicholas Roerich. His superb use of color reveals beyond question the opened eye of the seer, for his paintings glow with authentic visioning of the inner worlds. On viewing his master-pieces, many sensitives hear the harmonies which are as inseparable from them as sound is inseparable from the living colors of the soul-world. So when the biographers of Bach refer to him as the pre-eminent *tone-poet* they write more truly than they know.

With the inception of church music there was inaugurated the custom of portraying the Passion in its own musical setting on Good Friday. In the year 1729 Bach composed his *Passion* in accordance with the Gospel of St. Matthew. It was given its first presentation in Leipzig on Good Friday, April 15th of that year, under his own direction. He drew upon music of the Ancient Passion, which had been performed continuously in Leipzig churches since the early fifteenth century. Performers stood in the organ gallery in the western nave, *facing east*, women in the center and men on either side. The full story of the Passion is represented in a series of twelve pictures, or steps; twelve small ones represented by the chorals and twelve large ones by the arias.

The chorus typifies the voice of the people, namely, mass consciousness—the majority of whom, according to Paul, are able to receive only the *milk* of outer teachings. In the opening chorus is heard the restless, surging, uneasy soul motif by the masses as the hours of the Passion draw nigh.

Bach stands alone among master composers in his tone-painting of occult symbolism. His *Passion* begins with the anointing of the Master's feet with the precious essence from Mary's alabaster vase. Violins register the indignation of the onlookers and, later, the exquisite pathos and compassion of the Master's reply to their expostulations.

The Last Supper motif attains to heights of triumphant and upsweeping confidence, the confidence acquired through direct conscious experience of immortal life, interrupted by neither sleep nor death.

The Agony in Gethsemane is sublimely portrayed in the music *"Savior, bow before the Father."*; also the resignation voiced in the aria *"Let this cup pass"* yet *"not my will but thine."* The last words are literally sounded by an accompaniment of angelic voices, a direct transcription of celestial music.

Bach's genius for tone-painting was never more definitely evident than in the Judas aria now introduced: *"No price for murder paid, now in guilty tribute laid."* In solemn and awesome modulations the terrible karmic reaping is emphasized: *"The wheat brings forth no fruit, but it falls then to the earth."*

Part II begins the trial before the High Priest. The soul signature of the Christ is musically revealed in a glorious motif. The blindness and ignorance of the masses is vividly expressed by the passion and anger of the chorus as it shouts heartlessly, *"Crucify him!"*

Deep and solemn are the measures that accompany the Path of Sorrow, the Way of Calvary. The very air seems redolent with sadness, as though some mystic flower breathed out its fore-knowledge of the Crucifixion under the law of causation.

Three great musical scenes follow. In the first is shown the release of Barabbas, the scourging of Christ Jesus, His delivery to the cross. In the second is sensed His faltering steps, His falling under the cross, and the coming of Simon of Cyrene to His aid. Here is heard the exquisite *"Oh blessed cross, be mine to share it,"* which sounds the initiatory call to whomsoever will respond. The third scene is one of darkness, death, the ponderous tolling of bells. The music depicting the final scenes upon Calvary, the thunder and lightning and the rending of the veil, is agitated and heavy with fear, hatred, sorrow and all the other conflicting emotions of those standing by.

The gloomy scenes of Calvary are superseded by the glory of the Resurrection. Love and radiance illumine the heavens with the triumphant words, *"Behold, Jesus put forth His hand, giving the strength whereby we stand."* Bells of the Easter sunrise out-chime the funeral bells. Airy figures arise and ascend amid the golden chromatics of melody In music that is exultantly beautiful, Bach makes a triumphant declaration that, through liberation from the cross of matter, Christ Jesus is drawing all mankind unto Him.

This is the true meaning and purpose of Initiation. This is the paramount message, whether it be enunciated in poetry, painting, the power of the spoken word or music. Its media are many but its truth is one. In the stupendous music depicting the cosmic impulse released throughout earth with the sunrise of that Easter morn, the supreme genius of this master musician reaches its apex. In floods of scintillant glory it sweeps outward and upward until its listeners are transported into a rapture which unseals the ear of their souls and they hear the echoing and re-echoing of celestial choirs.

We may take it as axiomatic that the more powerful and far-reaching the message of a musical work, the more abstract is its esoteric symbolism. Also that the more deeply spiritual or abstract the message released by such a work, the closer it is attuned to those Akashic Records which were fashioned in the beginning by *tone*—that is, by the power of the initial Word. The New Age will be given a new science of musical esthetics developed along this line, a science in which the arts will be studied as correlatives of Initiation. Bach was a pioneer in this *Science of the Arts.*

* * *

When all is done and said, music remains alone in all the arts the perfect art: because it strikes the soul without the aid of the intellect. Music is common utterance of common emotion: the pouring forth of feeling unexplained: the voice of the heart within the heart: the sociable outburst of the barbarian—the immutable barbarian God made in the beginning: the undying thing in us all.
—William Kiddier

Wagner's *Tannhauser*

As the Autumn Equinox depicts the annual contest in nature between the powers of light and powers of darkness, so the story of *Tannhauser* depicts the mighty struggle in the life of every aspirant between the powers of his soul and the magnetic pull of the sense life— a conflict which finds its summary in the overture to the Wagnerian opera based on this rivalry. In the opera *Tannhauser,* which correlates with the Autumn Equinox, Wagner outlined tests and temptations that beset the path of a disciple as he endeavors to reach the goal of Purification, the keynote of this season.

The overture opens with strains from the *Pilgrim's Chorus.* This exquisite music is the underlying theme of the entire work, for it portrays musically the voice of conscience in the struggle between man's higher and lower natures. The same strains bring the opera to a glorious finale significant of the former's victory. This battle between *soul* and *sense* is a long and arduous ordeal familiar to every aspirant. Only through the strength of dedicated will can one achieve eventual mastery.

Early in the opera the Knight Tannhauser is found completely ensnared by the wiles of Venus, a situation dramatically scored in the stirringly sensuous *Venusberg* music, an interweaving of haunting phrases from the *Pilgrim's Chorus* with lilting measures ascribed to Venus and her realm of enchantment. Throughout the music one senses an attempt by each element to gain dominion over the aspiring Knight. He hears the chiming of church bells—ever symbolical of the call of spirit—and succeeds in wresting himself free from the spell of Venus, lure of the sense life, and calls upon the name of the Blessed Virgin.

From this point he determines to go forward upon the path of spiritual attainment, symbolized by his entrance into the Castle of the Wartberg to take part in a contest of song.

In the great hall where the contest is held, the opera again depicts man's higher and lower natures pitted against each other. Wolfram, a holy Knight who typifies the spiritual self, sings of an exalted love which unites soul to soul, such love as is a foretaste of the beautiful comradeship that will exist between men and women in the coming Aquarian Age. But Tannhauser, again under the spell of Venus and her sensual ecstasies, sings of that possessive lust-love which has ever brought sorrow, pain and tragedy to mortals during the present Piscean Age.

Following his wild outburst the Knight, once more overcome by grief because of his weakness and vacillation, joins a band of pilgrims. Strengthened by a new resolve—revealed in the musical theme of conscience, the *Pilgrims' Chorus*—he sets out for Rome to gain absolution.

In the final scene of the opera the entire landscape is shrouded in mist and one senses the melancholy mood of autumn. Dying leaves of crimson and gold fall upon the sorrowing Elizabeth, symbol of power through an awakened spirit, as she kneels before a statue of the Virgin seeking forgiveness for Tannhauser. In solemn cadence the *Pilgrims' Chorus* is now heard approaching from a distance.

Here follows a re-enactment of the conflict between the soul and the sense life. Wolfram describes in a veritable rhapsody of sound, the *Evening Star* aria, the supreme glory of the soul's oneness with God. In sharp contrast to this wondrous revelation of spirit's sublime attainment, Tannhauser enters, distraught and menacing, and declares in harsh and bitter tones that he has been denied absolution and is on his way back to the Venusberg. As he utters this threat he is surrounded by a lurid red light and Venus is heard calling to him in soft, caressing cadences.

In the midst of this dramatic situation sounds a sorrowful dirge. A procession appears, accompanying the body of the saintly Elizabeth on a bier. Tannhauser, now completely broken with remorse, turns his back on Venus and, in a frenzy of repentance, throws himself beside the bier. As he rededicates his life to the ways of spirit, the voice of Venus fades away singing, *"He is lost to me forever."* At this moment another band of pilgrims arrives bearing the rod of the Pope which has blossomed in token of forgiveness for Tannhauser. The great work concludes with the magnificent strains of the *Pilgrims' Chorus,* no longer sad and muted but joyous and triumphant.

Tannhauser is probably the most beautiful story of regeneration and transmutation to be found in all the annals of literature and music. Only through faith, persistence and perseverance can an aspirant gain the glorious soul-emancipation that comes with the triumph of spirit over the claims of sense, an emancipation that brings with it a revelation of love eternal and life immortal.

The color notes of this great music-seer, Richard Wagner, shine forth in a soft cast of mauve-purple together with a glittering radiance of white and gold.

CHAPTER X

The Winter Solstice

Schubert's *Ave Maria*
Wagner's *Lohengrin*

The Cosmic Nativity Song

he Winter Solstice begins on December 21 and reaches its climax of spiritual power at midnight of December 24, which date is known throughout the Christian world as Holy Night. The orthodox Christian at this time pays homage to the birth of the Christ Child in the little town of Bethlehem.

The mystic Christian, however, observes on this night a threefold devotion. He, too, pays homage to the birth of the Christ Child in Bethlehem. He also gives forth praise and thanksgiving for the awakening Christ Light which is being born within himself for if he lives to the highest that he knows this Christ Light is continuously growing in power and radiance throughout the years.

Finally, and most important of all, on this night he offers deference to the glorious radiant Christ Spirit, the highest Initiate of the archangelic Hosts, who is the Lord and Saviour of this entire Earth planet. It is on this night that He passes into the center or heart of this Earth in His work of regeneration and restoration that it may be lifted once again to its former high estate.

When the Lord Christ begins His annual descent into the earth

He touches its physical envelope at the time of the Autumn Equinox and during the days and weeks that follow He is continuously permeating every atom of this Earth with the wondrous magic of His Love and His Light and His Power. When at midnight of Holy Night He reaches the heart of the Earth, it is then, if one could view this planet from outer space, it would be seen as a radiant luminous ball filled with the glory Light which only the Love and Power of the Lord Christ could generate.

It is at the stroke of midnight of this Holy Time that a strange, wonderful peace and quiet suffuses the Earth for it is at this time that the Lord Christ is enfolding this planet and all the beings that live upon it with His all-encompassing Spirit and is pouring forth His universal benediction of love and good will. It is in this magic hour that hosts of Angels and Archangels are surrounding the Earth with triumphant chorusing, shedding their divine blessing upon it. And times without number the Lord Christ intones His most wonderful promise given to man: "Lo, I am with you always, even unto the end of the world."

Voice of Creation

Music is the harmonious voice of creation; an echo of the inner world; one note of the divine concord which the entire universe is destined one day to sound.

—*Mazzini*

The Earth Initiation whereby man learns the supreme Rite of Purification, or the conquest of spirit over matter, constitutes a part of the mystic ceremonial of the Winter Solstice Season. For the Initiate, the Nativity means the overcoming of the last enemy, Death, and a new birth into the glory of Immortal Life.

Those who attain to this sublime experience are eligible to take part with others of like Illumination in spiritualizing the atoms of this Earth planet. This work also constitutes a part of the Winter Solstice Ceremonial.

This spiritualizing process is accomplished largely by means of sound. The Christ Himself through His mighty Intonation gives the keynote of the Great Work. This Intonation corresponds to the word of St. John's Gospel by which all things are made. In other words, it was the initial musical Tone sounded forth by the Sun Spirit, the Christ, that built all the worlds of the solar system to which this Earth planet belongs. Thus He becomes truly the Lord and Saviour of this Earth before whom every knee must bow. His keynote it was that fashioned our planetary scheme, so consequently our evolutionary life is attuned to His Being in the most intimate sense. In Him we literally live and move and have our being.

The Four Sacred Seasons accentuate this Planetary Song. The tones of the Spring Equinox and the Summer Solstice are out-breathing in their action; they are radiating and building in quality. The tones of the Autumn Equinox and the Winter Solstice are in-breathing in their action; they are sustaining and enfolding.

The powerful Intonation or Word sounded cosmically at this season lifts and harmonizes every atom of the planet and is accompanied by such a mighty outburst of Light that all the world is enfolded in a divine radiance such as never yet lay on land or sea.

Multitudinous Hosts of higher Celestials together with resplendent arrays of Angels and Archangels all unite in this majestic chorus with our Lord until every animate thing, every tree of the forests and every minute growing plant sways and bends with the high ecstacy of music and light. Numerous and exquisite legends abound relative to the influence of the spiritual forces on the animal kingdom during this most gracious time. These legends all have their basis in fact, as animals are extremely sensitive to inner plane activities.

It is during the Winter Solstice Season that down through the ages, the Temple doors swing wide and when those who aspire to come into attunement with the Great Light of the world, have entered therein. To focus consciousness so completely in life as to harmonize every body-atom with the rhythms of the Christ Song, is the requirement essential for this entrance.

As the victorious one becomes increasingly absorbed in the Light Eternal, he begins to discern something of the words of the Planetary Song and listens to the supreme musical mantram to which this Earth planet it attuned. This Song is translated for human hearing in the words: "I am the way, the truth and the life."

During the Christmas season this supreme chant is lifted far up into the starry spaces by innumerable Hosts where their triumphant chorale is augumented by the voices of those belonging to our human life-wave who have attained unto this exalted state of consciousness.

The last enemy to be overcome is death. This truth has always been a Temple teaching, and is the goal of man's highest quest in the Initiation of the Winter Solstice. From the aureole of His transcendent glory, the Master who is our divine Life pattern bends low above us in this hallowed time and beckons us forward upon that Illumined Way, as all the Earth becomes resonant with the vast re-echoing music of His words that we shall all hear when we have made this high attainment our own: "Well done, thou good and faithful servant, enter into the joys of thy Lord."

The Healing Power of Schubert's "Ave Maria"

Music is the language of the heaven world. What form is to the physical world, color is to the astral world, and tone is to the next higher plane of consciousness, the World of Thought.

Music has the power of reaching the spirit of man more deeply than any other art and arousing it to a recollection of the spiritual world from which it came. It awakens a spiritual nostalgia. "Methinks I am never merry when I hear sweet music," says Jessica in a pensive love scene, to which Lorenzo, her lover, replies, "The reason is your spirits are attentive." In these simple lines Shakespeare points to an esoteric fact underlying a more or less common experience of everyone. A touch of sadness comes over a person who reflects on our present state in the light of musical intimations relative to that real world whereof our eternal self is native, but from which it is temporarily exiled.

Certain great composers have been, from time to time, caught up in a spirit of exaltation to communicate with the higher realms and hear what is known as *immortal music* because it will live as long as the earth planet endures. Much so-called Christmas music belongs in the same category. Various Christmas carols are direct transcriptions of angelic songs. Although transcribed during early Christian and medieval times, their beauty and inspiration have endured, and will most surely continue so to do throughout centuries to come.

Angelic music possesses dynamic healing power. That this is true of Schubert's *Ave Maria* is evidenced in an instance that occurred during World War II. A young soldier was wounded on a battlefield in Sicily. His condition was critical. By the time he arrived at a hospital in England it was found that his mind was completely clouded. His inhibitions appeared insurmountable. Though most doubtful, physicians and psychiatrists agreed that they might possibly be overcome if the patient could be moved to tears, but all their efforts to make him weep were unsuccessful.

Later, in an American hospital, the desired result was obtained by a quite unexpected means. The patient, handcuffed to two attendants, was taken into a concert room where he was exposed to the influence of an instrument that produced a combination of tone and color vibrations. The attendants were obliged to hold up his head and prop open his eyelids to make him see the screen presentation. As the reel unrolled, its magic spell caused his taut muscles and tense body to relax gradually. Then a miraculous thing happened.

The exquisite color-tone rendition of Schubert's *Ave Maria* flooded the screen and the boy began to weep. For twenty minutes his tears flowed without restraint. He was returned to his bed where he slept quietly for nine hours without the aid of sedation. Though he had been unable to speak or care for himself in any way since his injury, he was quiet and entirely rational at the end of that period. He woke up and said most naturally, "I have just awakened." and he *had*!

The *Ave Maria* of Schubert is a transcription of the Blessed Virgin's musical soul-pattern. It vibrates to the keynote of that Holy One whose ministry to man centers on healing and regeneration. In the composer's lovely music her powers of love and healing pour forth. No one can listen to it without being enfolded in a wave of its spiritual harmony. If one is conscious of its healing power, and knows it for what it is, it will add greatly to one's capacity for receiving its divine remedial benefits.

Franz Schubert's color-note is a lovely intermingling of white and silver.

Wagner's "Lohengrin"

Aptly, the Winter Solstice has been referred to as "An observance looking toward the coming of the Great Light." As far back as is known this season has been celebrated by a ritual called the Vigil of the Light, wherein assembled multitudes knelt in adoration before blazing luminants of one type or another. The first observances were conducted in caves or mounds; later, these gave way to Temples; but always there were lights and a midnight vigil of adoration.

Since the dawn of civilization high priests have gathered their disciples about them and secretly taught of the coming of the Great Light, the one who was to be the Light of the World. Century after century there has run through every racial folklore and every religious creed this secret teaching like a golden thread. Each civilization has made preparations for the coming of the Supreme Light, connecting it with a celebration of the Winter Solstice.

With the advent of the Lord Christ this observance became the Christ-Mass. His incarnation was the most momentous of all world events. So important was it that the passage of time is still divided into B.C., before Christ, and A.D., after Christ.

On the night of the first Christ-Mass the Christ Ray was focused upon Earth until the entire planet became luminous, as hosts of celestial Beings winged their way through the physical and spiritual realms heralding the coming of the World Redeemer. . .

Upon this Holy Night the radiant Angel Gabriel assumes guardianship of our earthly sphere and of all its activities for the winter quarter of the year. Gabriel is the Angel assigned to mothers and children. At this time he and the Blessed Virgin bestow a tender benediction upon prospective mothers and those egos who will incarnate during the coming year. Truly, it is a magic night, one dedicated to mothers and children.

Also, upon Holy Night the doors to the Mystery Temples are

opened to all who are worthy to enter. The Christian Mystery Temple is located in the ethers above the Holy Land. There it is that Mary, Joseph and the first Disciples still meet to pour out their blessing upon mankind. Every organization, church congregation, consecrated group or individual that spends this period in devout prayer and meditation receive a blessing through the divine energies that stream into the earth from this Mystery Temple on high.

Then it is that a worthy aspirant is permitted to pass into the presence of the Lord Christ. Caught up momentarily, he becomes one with the Light of the World. After this transcendent experience the successful candidate is a changed person. Personality is conquered, leaving only the divine selfhood. Upon him is impressed the very signature of the Christ. Should someone smite him on one cheek he will turn the other. Should he be asked for his coat he will give also his cloak. If called upon to go one mile he will go two. His whole aim in life is to give himself in loving, self-forgetting service wheresoever needed, for in that moment of at-one-ment he has learned that all life is sacred, that to hurt one is to hurt all and to serve one is to serve all. He has transferred his point of focus from the finite to the infinite, from the temporal to the eternal, and in soul ecstasy found the Allness of the One and the Oneness of the All.

The exquisite legend of Lohengrin could be subtitled "The Coming of the Light," for Lohengrin typifies those compassionate beings who, having been reborn, dedicate themselves completely to the service of others. These emancipated souls oftentimes renounce a merited heaven-life to remain within astral realms so they can minister to those in the agony of earthbound purgation.

Such is Elsa in the Lohengrin narrative. She has reached an advanced state of consciousness, having developed the power of conscious invisible helpership. She is able to bridge the interval between passing into sleep and returning to wakefulness, and thus brings back into awareness a memory of her inner-world experiences. During her hours of sleep she is instructed by her Teacher, the chaste and beautiful White Knight Lohengrin. Elsa's entrance into the Temple accompanied by the knight symbolizes the passing of an illumined aspirant into the Hall of the Mysteries, to stand in the presence of the Christ. With the aid of Lohengrin, Elsa is able to pass into the Temple; but she falters before the subtle test which is to prove whether she is worthy to know his name, which, bearing his soul signature, would reveal to her his true spiritual status.

Many there are who have attained to such a high estate and then been unable to go further. And many have been the Initiate-teachers who have descended to earth only to be repudiated and betrayed. As the poet so graphically expresses this tragic fact, "For Socrates, the hemlock; for Christ, Gethsemane," while the New Testament states, "He came unto his own, and his own received him not." The tragedy and pathos of this knowledge, all its sadness and its longing, are expressed in the ineffable Wagnerian music of Lohengrin's swan song. Yet, despite the failures of mankind, each Teacher who has descended to earth has promised to return again at a more auspicious time, for the failures and weaknesses of one life can be stepping stones and a source of strength and aspiration, in another. Richard Wagner himself declared that "Elsa will in time rise up to Lohengrin through rebirth."

Year after year, at the time of the Winter Solstice, and as light and love pour forth from the Christ and from centers in the earth, the planet is being cleansed and leavened. Eventually its rhythms will be so accelerated that man can no longer hate his fellow man or destroy him by the atrocities of war. Comes a glad day when there will be no divisions into nations and races—but the unity of one vast brotherhood. Then there will be no more sorrow at the parting called death, no more pain or disease—for, as John describes his vision, the former things will have passed away. This will be the heralded New Day that presages the second coming of the Christ.

Hosts of Angels and Archangels descend to earth at the holy Christmas Season, chanting of that New Day to come. The keynote of the planet is attuned to their Christmas anthem: *"Glory to God in the highest and on earth peace, goodwill to men."* As they flood the ethers with their song each year, the wonder of its fruition draws closer to fulfillment. And amidst the magic of color and beauty, of happiness and song, sounds the triumphant intonation of the Blessed Lord Himself:

I am come that they might have life
And have it more abundantly.

PART V

NATURE'S INNER PLANE CEREMONIALS

CHAPTER XI

Sunrise and Sunset in a Desert Sanctuary

Music always around me, unceasing
Unbeginning—yet long untaught I
did not hear,
But now I hear and am elated.
—*Walt Whitman*

All that takes place in nature is permeated with a mysterious
music which is the earthly projection of the music of the spheres.
In every plant and in every animal there is really incorporated a
tone of the music of the spheres.
—*Rudolf Steiner*

alm, mysterious, brooding, the desert stretches out toward infinity, ever overshadowed by a benediction of peace. Such is the picture that meets one's objective vision. But when the veil between inner and outer realms is rent, what appeared as brooding silence is transformed into rhythms of intense activity.

* * *

Dawn came and along the horizon appeared a faint line of delicate mauve-pink, barely perceptible and melting into purple tones on the desert floor. As morning became more clearly defined this line expanded until the very atmosphere was suffused with brilliant rose-pink.

119

Then it was that something very wonderful happened. Against the shining horizon appeared an endless procession of celestial Presences. During the hush they seemed absorbed in some profound and prayerful meditation. The result of this period became apparent in great undulating waves of golden light which emanated from these glorious Presences and suffused the desert air with streamers of force.

Some of the bright Beings then floated majestically above the desert sands and assembled in groups of twelve over certain areas. Once again their combined meditative prayer resulted in a veritable down-pouring of golden light, this time limited to each group's particular area.

While observing the sunrise we noted a settler's cabin had been built in the very center of one such down-pouring, and we wondered if this had been done by a person who "sees" or if the owner was so insensate as to live in the midst of such power and yet be oblivious of it.

If man could be blind to the wonders about him, the innumerable hosts of nature spirits were not. In troops and processions, these little creatures approached with reverence those golden light centers to take in as much as they could of the radiant life force. Then they poured it into the roots of plants and shrubs with which they were working.

The rose-pink lines along the horizon changed into molten gold. With the appearance of the Sun there passed through the heart of the desert a thrill of almost divine ecstasy. Birds trilled in higher accords of harmony while supernatural Beings, from nature spirits to the celestial Presences, bowed down in homage before its glory.

As the Sun's rays rose higher the glowing Presences disappeared into its radiant shining, and the desert, quiet, mysterious yet vibrant with deep contentment, lay waiting the miracle of another dawn. An unidentified writer has significantly expressed his concept of this phenomenon: ". . . an ego swathed in its own conceits and consecrated to veneration of its own superiority must flee before the timeless immensity of a desert dawn or dusk."

Every event of the day is attuned to its own particular tone-pattern. Each morning, when the Sun rises above the desert horizon in a burst of golden glory, may be heard a vibrant symphony of the tone-pattern of the day. With the sinking of the Sun below the horizon, the desert is enfolded in glowing streamers of crimson, purple and gold like a rainbow of blessings. Then there sounds forth in soft and dulcet strains a recapitulation of the day's tone-pattern. Thus the sunrise and the sunset over the desert create a color-symphony which exceeds all others in variety and magnificence. But only in the hushed calm of a hallowed sanctuary can its musical tones become clearly audible.

CHAPTER XII

Twilight Symphony Of the Sea

hat such beings as undines or water sprites actually exist is given but slight credence in our matter-of-fact world. Nevertheless the fact remains that, despite our lack of vision and dullness of comprehension, we may see a glorious panorama of one of nature's ceremonials if we gaze out to sea at twilight. Undines are rightly called *spirits of the sea* for they embody its very elements in their make-up. Their lithesome motions and lilting songs are a harmonious blending of the melodic sweep and rhythm of incoming breakers.

Undines are seldom seen in the surf as it breaks upon the shore. They give the impression of being shy and of shunning such human noises as shouting and loud laughter. Therefore, the most propitious hour for enjoying their revelling is the twilight hour when beaches are sometimes deserted and quiet. Then it is that as far as eye can see these minute creatures come riding the foaming crest of waves, and looking like an exquisite blend of gleaming water and sunlit air.

Sylphs, spirits of the air, are so in harmony with the undines that, in shining companies, they float just above the waves and in perfect rhythm with the undines. The ensemble of sylphs and undines, silhouetted against the golden glow of the departing sun and the pink-mauve shadows of descending twilight, forms a heavenly etching. Scenes such as this await the inspiration of a New Age artist blessed with eyes that truly see.

There are enchanting legends concerning the undines. It is

122

related that only a gossamer foam of light is left shining on the sea at the expiration of their life term—which generally extends to several hundred years of our time. But if an undine is beloved of a mortal, then part of the mortal's soul is given to it and it thus is endowed with immortality. Fact and fancy are strangely interwoven. The eventual heritage of every undine must be immortality because they are the essence of beauty, and beauty is the innermost heart of Truth which is ever immortal.

The song of the undines are attuned to the rhythm of the tides. Their voices are so soft and low that they merge into the louder sounds of the sea. Once heard, however, they can never be forgotten. Because their songs are so plaintive, so hauntingly tender, the memory of them lingers in one's heart forever, like some cherished dream.

CHAPTER XIII

A Tryst With Spring

o the degree that man attunes himself with nature's processes does his wisdom increase. Busily engaged in objective activities and enmeshed in worldly interests, the mortal is rare indeed who takes time to cultivate that unworldly reverence which opens doors upon spiritual vision and knowledge.

When the new Sun is born at the Winter Solstice, the sublime symphony of spring begins to reverberate in the heart of earth. This ecstatic rhapsody awakens the plant kingdom from its post-harvest slumber and, by its vibrant and harmonious pulsation, causes sap to ascend, buds to form and burst. The symphony flows out in subdued tones during the month of January, its cadences barely audible. These become more modulated during February and then the music can be clearly heard. In March the modulations increase, each tonal measure being fraught with new power. All nature vibrates with activity and is redolent with beauty and fragrance. By the arrival of the Spring Equinox the symphony has attained to its climactic splendor.

The oft-heard expression "Spring is in the air" has a profound occult significance for the mystic. He sees more than the bare, bleak trees beheld by earth-dulled eyes. Early in February, as a reflex from spring's symphony, a mist of color arises from the soil and enfolds each tree and plant in luminous veils of softest pink, silver and green. Ancient Temple neophytes were taught to use these waves of spring-tide color for renewing and revitalizing their

124

life force, with the result that a long life and abounding health were their natural heritage. The urge to commune with nature remains with us as part of this half-forgotten practice.

The *little folk* are such an important and fascinating feature of a tryst with spring. Minute, ethereal, delicate and lovely, they appear and disappear like some airy fantasy. Shrouding themselves in veils of the soft color-mist which arises from the earth, they busy themselves at embellishing etheric archetypes of the plant kingdom. Trees and shrubs are surrounded with an etheric prototype as nature spirits adorn them with a shimmer of sheerest pink that later melts into silver and finally merges into the softest green.

The bright messengers of light whom we call Angels influence and control the inner workings of nature. The *little folk* act entirely under their direction. These wee beings seem to work in relays. They come in processionals, presenting themselves before the Angels who bless them for their forthcoming activity. As the Angels breathe upon each fairy worker it instantly shines forth in the color with which it is to operate. Angels think and speak in color and, by some undefined alchemy, endow their charges with ability to work with a specific vibratory tint.

In our tryst with spring we noted a wild peach tree adorned with clusters of pink-and-white blossoms. As the Angels blessed each tiny worker, its robe assumed tones of the same pink and white, and it went unerringly to poise itself gracefully upon a flower petal bearing its own distinctive hues.

When the Angel of Spring sounds the spiritual keynote, the life force which has slept during the winter months in the roots and bulbs of trees and plants awakens and begins its upward climb toward their topmost crest. This spiralling motion, all out-weaving and out-flowing, strong, right and enthusiastic with all the glory of incoming springtide, is attuned in its song to major notes.

The motions and appearance of both Angels and nature spirits are in complete accord with the glorious symphony of nature that becomes clearer and more powerful as the season advances. Finally the etheric pattern for the whole plant kingdom is complete. The forces released by the pattern then merge with the outer physical forms of tree and vine, of shrub and plant. Not until this takes place does insensate man become aware of the miracle of spring.

When the Angel of Autumn sounds the spiritual keynote, the life force throughout the Plant Kingdom begins again its spiralling descent toward roots and bulbs for its long winter sleep. This spiralling descent is attuned to minor notes as though filled with a soft and tender melancholy.

Thus it is that the passing months are filled with the beautiful symphonies of the seasons in all the exquisiteness of their color and tone. However, all this beauty is still unseen by the eyes and unheard by the ears of the great majority of present-day humanity.

CHAPTER XIV

Autumn—The Sacrificial Song

utumn has long been regarded as the sacrificial season. It is for this reason we have entitled the autumn song the Song of Sacrifice. It is in this season that all nature is tremulous, tender, melancholy as though grieving over the last vestiges of summer's waning beauty.

It is in this season that the Lord Christ renounces the glory of the high celestial realms and descends to incarcerate himself in the heart of the earth for the next six months which is a part of His annual sacrifice for the upliftment and betterment of all the life waves evolving upon this planet. His sacrifice was not made just once for all time but is an annual offering which He will continue to make until all mankind has been redeemed. It is for this reason that autumn time is known as the Season of the Cosmic Crucifixion.

It is also in this season that Michael, the luminous Archangel, accompanied by his hosts of attending Angels returns to this physical plane to also bestow His benediction upon the earth and its humanity.

Each year mankind through its evil thoughts and deeds generates a dark miasmic cloud that hovers over the planet. A part of the autumnal work of Michael and His Angels is to dissolve this evil cloud and so enable man to renew, rebuild and purify his own desire body by means of finer astral substance. Thus each year this mighty Archangel accelerates immeasurably the evolutionary progress of all humanity.

This is also the most fitting season of the year for the aspirant who aims to walk in the Christ way to make his dedication to the Path. This is also the most propitious time for those who have been long on the Way to renew and reconsecrate themselves to walk more closely in the footsteps of Christ and to live more nearly in accord with His precepts as enunciated in the Sermon on the Mount. This is also the season calling for the renunciation of the things which stand in the way of living for the life of the spirit. For those who are persistent and faithful in heeding the call of the spirit to come up higher will eventually be found worthy to enter into the very presence of the Lord Christ Himself and to partake of the true Christ-Mass that lies at the heart of the festive Christmas season.

CHAPTER XV

The Redwood Forest—God's Own Cathedral

In every giant trunk an epic lies,
A psalm in every branch that scales the skies.

t was long ago, many centuries before secular history began its record, that the great redwood forests were charged with mighty spiritual impulses which have caused them, even to this day, to be powerful centers of magnetic force. This work was accomplished by the great Overlords of Destiny when they ordained these magnificent trees to become primitive man's first temples of worship. The consecrated areas where they grew furnished a blue-print for the majestic old world cathedrals that were to come later.

In common with all other physical manifestations, the big trees have both an inner and outer life and activity. Their outer or objective life, with its stately magnificence, is viewed annually by thousands upon thousands of visitors filled with awed admiration. Their inner life and activities are revealed to those only who have transcendent sight and hearing.

So long have nature's Titans been beneficent servers in the evolutionary scheme that, in common with all else centered in the All Good, they created for themselves no means of self-defense. Yet they continue relatively unharmed. Even forest fires fail to destroy them. Furthermore, despite his many and wide-spread depredations in the realm of nature, man has been moved to set them apart as protected sanctuaries. They have evolved no thorns,

129

spikes or prickers. Even their needle-shaped leaves are smooth and soft—as all will attest who have laid down to rest in their cushioned shadows.

The spiritual emanations from these mighty forest giants are so strong that reptiles and other noxious forms of life are repelled by the radiations of their bright auras, while deer and other harmless creatures seek these towering and peacefully assuring friends for protection. Birds seem to sense the sacredness of their cathedral-like atmosphere, for their songs are muted and reverent. Amid the vastness of the forest's leafy aisles one never hears the unrestrained outbursts of song which characterizes the bird life of other forests.

The spirit of devotion that seems to fairly envelope the feathered population of the redwoods is in perfect harmony with that of the Tree-Angels. These benign beings are tender and gracious with all that enters their environment, for they are the very essence of joy and love and service. When any creature, be it man or animal, senses something of the sacred aura of their gigantic charges, these Angels evince great pleasure and send forth a radiant blessing in return. If those who give expression to unseemly language or boisterous laughter in the presence of these Tree-Angels could see the sadness and hurt it brings them, they would bow low in humility and contrition.

The golden Tree-Angels are mellow with wisdom, not with age—although they have presided over the evolution of their majestic charges since the prehistoric days when, as mere tender shoots, they were reaching upward to catch the rays of the rising sun. The entire cycle of their inner and outer unfoldment is under this angelic guidance.

A most enthralling sight is that of the towering forest kings right after a storm when all their branches are weighted with millions of raindrops sparkling like innumerable diamonds. In the center of each glistening drop is a wee water sprite, exquisite in proportions and grace of movement, dancing in an utter abandonment of joy. Their every gesture is in accurate attunement to the rhythmic keynote of the lovely Angels who hover in tender benediction over the enchanting scene.

Upon reaching a certain stage of individualization, every tree is given into the care of a tree spirit. On every plane of existence the law holds that the highest degree of perfection is attained only by service. So to contact Tree-Angels who have rendered centuries of ministry as tree custodians, is a starred event in one's life, a milestone in the ever-lengthening corridors of memory. No artist has ever depicted on the face of the Messiah the infinite tenderness and compassion to be seen on the countenances of these angelic beings. With the exaltation of communion with them comes a sense of having been lifted into that realm where abides the peace which passeth understanding.

There is a certain area in this land of enchantment where a person may stand in the presence of the awe-inspiring mother-tree of the forest. The sublime "Madonna of the Redwoods" is seventy feet in diameter at the ground level and lifts its spine-adorned crest three hundred and twenty-nine feet heavenward to commune with the stars. It is a power center, sending out rays of energy that vibrate to the end of the earth. An observer who has learned to pass beyond the veils of sound and to shut out the distractions of mortal hearing will be conscious of rhythms of an exquisite chanting. They are the soft intoning of the mother Tree-Angel as she sends forth her blessings to mothers in all the world and to all those who are mothers yet to be.

Near this area stands the majestic Cathedral Group. The shadowed aisles and changing lights of such groups have been an inspiration to cathedral builders throughout the ages. Those who christened the redwood shrines were either consciously or unconsciouly imbued with the emanations from them, so fitting is the particular designation given to each one.

The early morning hours are the most inspirational for attending services in a redwood cathedral. Then it is that the heavenly chorus is clearly audible. A rare ecstasy animates the dawn matins, an ecstasy that etheric choristers echo and re-echo back and forth like the dulcet tones of far-away flutes. If these celestial hymns could be transcribed into earthly notes, the music would sound strangely like "Holy, holy, holy, descend O Lord of love and peace."

A short distance from the Cathedral Group is the Resurrection Tree. Here the vibrations are no longer subdued. They are vibrant, sparkling with a new life. The magnetic force rayed from it is a soothing balm to tired nerves and weary minds. It is healing and restoring in its effect. The voice of this mighty Tree-Angel seems to proclaim: "I am the resurrection and the life."

Each year since the event of Christ's Resurrection, the all-embracing radiation of His Cosmic Being has permeated the entire earth, growing more potent with each passing twelve-month. Two thousand years ago both men and Angels chanted this divine assertion. Now, alas, the majority of mankind has forgotten the words and their significance. Not so the Angels! They live, move and have their being in full realization of eternal life. In this consciousness they garner and utilize the new life force released by our Blessed Lord each year, doing so in a manner unknown to man. Mighty is the healing power evoked by Angels in their unceasing chant: "I am the resurrection and the life."

Composers of organ music, such as Johann Sebastian Bach and Caesar Franck, must have transcribed for humanity the music of their own mystical woodlands, for their music seems to be climaxed by the soul-songs of celestial Presences who preside over the activities of both individual trees and whole forests.

A great silence broods over the mystic redwoods. Radiations of the mother Tree-Angel are made luminous by golden lights that flash in and out of the cathedral-like aisles, fairy fantasies of unspeakable beauty. This divine Being gathers up all sounds of joy or sorrow, of rebellion or resignation, that have registered in the atmosphere of the giant forest sentinels during their existence. These are then woven into a vast veil of silence which drapes itself over the entire environment. The veil of silence becomes the voice of wisdom for those who can interpret its unspoken message. This it is that accounts for a sudden sense of awe and reverence which enfolds even the uninitiated upon entering the sacred precinct.

PART VI

SOME OCCULT EFFECTS OF MUSIC

CHAPTER XVI

Studies in Reactions to Wagner's "Valkyrie"

ith permission we reprint an article by Marie Russak that appeared the *The American Theosophist,* not so much for the factual data it contains, interesting and important as this is, as for the realms of unexplored phenomena on which it lifts the veil and the power which music in general, and in this instance, Wagner's in particular, exercises over human life and consciousness, even though we may be completely unaware of its effects beyond the generally experienced emotional and mental reactions. Marie Russak was one of the most advanced of Madame Blavatsky's disciples.

In the December issue of the English Vahan there was a criticism (signed Adsocius Novus) of Mr. Jinarajadasa's lecture on *The Aesthetic Value of Music.* I am glad to be able to feel heartily in sympathy with Mr. Jinarajadasa's ideas on the subject and perhaps Adsocius Novus might be interested in the following:

Some years ago I made a few investigations into the hidden side of music and at that time I had occasion to attend a series of performances of Richard Wagner's *Der Ring des Nibelungen,* given at the Opera in Dresden. The opportunity was seized to watch the effect of the music upon the subtler bodies of some of those present—a perfectly legitimate thing to do, since the people were strangers and the investigation made with the motive of gaining knowledge, not for curiosity but to help others. The following is from the notes written at the time.

At the performances mentioned I noticed particularly three

people who sat in front of me; a young lady aged about seventeen, an old gentlemen about sixty, evidently her father, and a gentlemen about thirty-five.

Case I

The young lady. Before the performance began she seemed rather listless and indifferent. The health aura showed signs of delicate health. The astral body was full of the usual colors, with signs here and there of irritation, probably from the excitement of the average person incidental to the preparations for such an evening and getting to the opera. Her mental body was replete with thought-forms of music, and it later developed that she was a musical student who had spent the afternoon studying the score of the opera to be given in the evening. (Note this fact especially.)

Before the first act was half over a great difference in her health aura was noticed; it now glowed and scintillated with new vigor and it seemed to have been stimulated to a sufficiently high rate of vibration—a sort of psychological point—at which it was able to respond to an inner vitality or force which filled it with new strength.

Some curious phenomena in the bodies of the young lady now presented themselves. I noticed some streams of light protruding from her mental body like long, waving tentacles: on the end of each was a spinning thought-form similar to a vortex-like whirlpool in water, caused by suction. As some familiar motif floated up from the general vibrations of the music (coupled with the forms which were caused on the mental and astral planes in general in the room) these tentacles in her mental body sucked the vibrations into themselves in large proportions. They seemed to recognize and to become a part of each other. Other mental bodies near the young lady had few or none of these tentacles: therefore the effect on their mental bodies was practically nil, and the results in them of the vibrations from the music were more emotional than mental.

As the young lady's mental body drank in the thought-forms of the music the effect on it was most beautiful. The thought-forms already there, from the previous study of music, were strengthened until they filled the body with beautiful light. It seemed to relate her to the deep pulsations of the Law of Rhythm in all nature, and the experience made the separating walls (the vibratory difference) between the lower and higher mental bodies to disappear and the ego was able to approach nearer to the personality and to impress it with the loftiest ideas. The effect on the casual body was marked, and could never be lost, since it expanded, and when this happens it never returns to its former size.

What was the effect on the astral body? As the emotion caused by the understanding of the music and the appreciation of its beauty grew upon her mentally, the vibrations penetrated deeply to the astral body. It was not very long ere it was a great boiling mass of beautiful color—a mighty many-hued bird beating its wings against a cramped cage to escape. The vibrations from the color did escape, some of them, and spread out in all directions: like clouds of colored steam, but there was a kind of core which seemed to be a prisoner within the particularized radius of the astral body: it beat against its confines until it finally found an outlet: it found its way of least resistance and rushed through that—into tears. In most people, those who have no lower channels into which it can penetrate, while endeavoring to escape, will either laugh or cry: the young girl wept violently for awhile, until some of the pressure of it was exhausted, then she grew calm and for the rest of the evening was benefitted—in fact, she was a "new being" when she left the hall, in comparison to what she was when she entered it. The beneficial vibrations in her bodies (even if she experienced none such for many days to come) would continue to persist, unless some violent or astral emotion of another sort was experienced. Before leaving this case I would like to mention that if persons could see the amount of physical force that escapes with tears they might be less prone to shed them.

Case II

The gentleman of about sixty years evidently the young lady's father. His physical etheric looked well enough. The astral body was not unusual. He was evidently a Catholic—a very devout one—as there was a strong thought-form within his mental body of the crucifix, and I saw between the acts that a small gold cross hung from his watch-chain. He was also an artist for there were thought-pictures all around him of heads, landscapes and other such mental "sign-posts." His appreciation of the opera expressed itself mentally in admiration for the form, the colors, the pictures. The astral effect exhausted itself along the line of least resistance, which was his love for his daughter. As the music continued, great waves of force, and clouds of gorgeous pinks and blues went out from him and wound themselves around his daughter, as he held her hand tightly clasped in his: the force of his vibration added to her own, helped to lift her to heights she could not otherwise have reached. Towards the end of the opera the vibrations of the music had penetrated to the highest reaches of his being when he finally closed his eyes and clasped his hands as though in prayer. Then the beautiful waves of color also wound themselves around the thought form of the crucifix, showing that he was also religiously exalted as he listened to the wonderful closing orchestration of the fire music in *Die Walkure*. When he rose from his seat to leave the opera, his face aglow with a beautiful inner radiance as he said in charming, simple faith to his daughter: "How wonderfully kind is our God to give us such enjoyment in our world."

Case III

The man of about thirty-five is not such a happy one to describe. His physical-etheric body showed him to be in good health. Astrally he left much to be desired and the three lower planes of that body were over-developed by excesses of many kinds. There was much depression in evidence, and irritability. In his mental body there was a strong picture of a woman—I afterwards recognized it as the likeness of one of the leading singers of the evening. As the opera progressed, the changes in his bodies and the effect upon them was very marked. The first of these was on the astral body, and the vibrations of the music seemed to irritate him: he became very restless and the depression increased. This continued until the lady in whom he was interested came on the stage. The thought-form of her became clearer and clearer, and then the woman and the music were blended in a sweep of vibrations almost wholly astral and extremely detrimental to her. The clouds of color expressing passion and selfishness were most unpleasant to behold and, as the way of least resistance for him was along the line of lower excesses, he really seemed a victim to his lower nature. At the end of the first act he was forced to go out and get some strong drink which, perhaps, he thought would help him, but it only made matters worse for some time. By the end of the opera, however, the emotion had somewhat worn itself out, so to speak, and it was followed by a strong physical exhaustion. I wondered if, after all, he were not to derive some good from the beautiful music and by the witnessing of such art. I was not disappointed when I looked finally at the higher bodies. There had been, even in his case, what we may call a superconscious effect. There was, of course, a plane in his higher bodies to which the vibrations had penetrated of themselves and had produced the effect of bringing about the possibility of experiencing *consciously*, at some time in the future, the wonder of the great *Law of Rhythm*. They had deposited a seed, as it were, and this takes place each time one is in the vibrations which arise from such music.

These and later experiments have proven that in about seven cases out of ten the ethical effect of music is immediate and beneficial and that the immediate effect on the person depends entirely upon the condition of the bodies it contacts—the temperament of the person. Students of the occult should understand the inestimable value and place of all phases of emotion in our evolution.

There were some other musical experiments made in Budapest when I watched the effect of the music of a wild Hungarian gypsy band on the nature spirits. Each of the seven primal keynotes seemed to bring forth some one predominant color, and the expression of some one sentiment in these elementals. I have not touched upon the wonderful power as an occult assistance of the vibrations from music in certain keys, when the key is found to correspond to the tonal or numerical value of the person. But they are fascinating by-paths and foreign to these general hints.